T0305837

Corporate Policies
in a World with
Information Asymmetry

Corporate Policies
in a World with
Information Asymmetry

Vipin K Agrawal
University of Texas at San Antonio, USA

Ramesh K S Rao
University of Texas at Austin, USA

World Scientific

ICP Imperial College Press

Published by

World Scientific Publishing Co. Pte. Ltd.
5 Toh Tuck Link, Singapore 596224
USA office: 27 Warren Street, Suite 401-402, Hackensack, NJ 07601
UK office: 57 Shelton Street, Covent Garden, London WC2H 9HE

Library of Congress Cataloging-in-Publication Data
Agrawal, Vipin K.
   Corporate policies in a world with information asymmetry / by Vipin K. Agrawal (University of
Texas at San Antonio, USA) & Ramesh K.S. Rao (University of Texas at Austin, USA).
    pages cm
   Includes bibliographical references and index.
   ISBN 978-9814551304 (alk. paper)
   1. Corporations--Finance. 2. Dividends. I. Rao, Ramesh K. S. II. Title.
   HG4026.A364 2015
   658.15'224--dc23
                                        2015009076

British Library Cataloguing-in-Publication Data
A catalogue record for this book is available from the British Library.

In-house Editors: Lum Pui Yee/Dipasri Sardar

Typeset by Stallion Press
Email: enquiries@stallionpress.com

Printed in Singapore

This book is dedicated to:

Poonam, Pushpa, and Vijay
VA

Anita and Nikhil
RKSR

Acknowledgment

We would like to express our thanks to Dr. Zvi G. Ruder for encouraging us to write this book. We would also like to thank the editors at World Scientific — Ms. Monica Lesmana, Ms. Philly Lim, Ms. Pui Yee Lum and Ms. Dipasri Sardar for editorial assistance.

Contents

Part I

Introduction

I.1. Background

All economic activity originates at the primitive level of a transaction between two or more parties. The terms of these transactions depend on the amount of relevant information these two parties have. Further, an empirical reality is that one party typically possesses more information than the other, that is, there is informational asymmetry (IA). Over the past four decades the literature in economics and finance has recognized this reality and has asked: How does IA affect the way business is conducted?

This fundamental question has been studied in myriad settings (e.g., education, efficiency wage theory, credit rationing, organizational design, macroeconomics) and, recently, the contributions of George Akerlof, Michael Spence, and Joseph Stiglitz in this area earned them a Nobel Prize in economics. The research on this topic has: (i) demonstrated that IA can lead to inefficiencies in a transaction and (ii) examined ways in which these inefficiencies can be minimized.

To illustrate the nature of some of the problems arising from IA, consider the used cars market which was examined by George Akerlof in the classic 1970 paper titled "The Market for 'Lemons:' Quality Uncertainty and the Market Mechanism." Suppose, for simplicity, that there are two types of cars — half are of good quality (each worth $5,000) and half are of bad quality (each worth $1,000). There is *IA* in this market in the sense that whereas the seller of a used car knows whether the car is good or bad the buyer does not — the buyer only knows that there is a 50% chance that the car is good and a 50% chance that it is bad. Clearly, the buyer will only make an offer between $1,000 (the value of the car if it is bad) and $5,000 (the value of the car if it is good). Now, suppose that the buyer offers $3,000. The seller will reject the offer if the car is a good car and will accept the offer if it is a bad one. In this situation, the buyer will get a car worth $1,000 and will therefore lose. In fact, the only price that the buyer can offer without over-paying is $1,000 and, in this situation, the seller will sell him the car only if it is a bad one. Thus, because of *IA* between the buyer and the seller, the only cars that will end up being sold in the used car market are the bad ones (the "lemons"). The market for good used cars will disappear. Such a market is clearly not desirable. The research has identified mechanisms to mitigate this problem (e.g., having an authorized mechanic check the car and provide a warranty on some parts, such as the AC unit).

This simple example of *IA* in the used cars market can be extended to an analysis of financial decisions that the manager of a publicly-traded corporation faces when he has to raise external capital. We elaborate on this below.

A corporate manager typically oversees several ongoing projects and has the opportunity to invest in new projects that add wealth to the stockholders. Such new projects include expanding the corporation's existing business, entering into a new line of business, acquiring another business, and so on. If the firm does not have sufficient internal capital (cash) to finance the initial investment, the manager must enter into a transaction with outside investors to raise the additional funds ("raising capital").

In this situation, the manager of a public corporation faces two key decisions:

(i) **Should** he transact with outside investors and raise the necessary capital to invest in the project? The answer to this question determines the firm's **investment policy**.

(ii) If the manager decides to raise external capital, **how** should the investment be financed — with debt, with equity, or with some other security? The answer determines the firm's **financing policy**.

Modern corporate finance theory, originating in 1958 with the seminal work of Merton Miller and Franco Modigliani, has studied these decisions in a world where outside (new) investors and the firm's manager have the same information about the firm — a world with "symmetric information." In this world, managerial decisions are fairly straight-forward: (i) the manager will raise the necessary capital and invest in the positive-*NPV* project since there is no cost/benefit to raising external capital and (ii) it does not matter how the investment is financed because cost of external financing is zero regardless of the financing choice. Thus, the firm's investment policy is simply to invest in all positive-*NPV* projects and financing policy is irrelevant.

In 1984, in a very influential paper in finance, Stewart Myers and Nicholas Majluf argued that these decisions become complicated when managers possesses more information about the firm than do the outside investors — that is, when there is *IA*. They demonstrated that *IA* can lead to a cost when raising external capital and hence to investment inefficiencies (i.e., positive-*NPV* projects may not get accepted by the manager). Further, they found that the firm can minimize this inefficiency (cost) through financing policy. Specifically, they found that firms can reduce the cost by following what finance researchers and textbooks commonly refer to as the pecking order theory — in raising capital, a firm first issues the least risky security, then the second least risky security, and so on. This implies that if, for exogenous reasons, only debt and equity can be issued, the firm will prefer debt over equity.

I.2. Motivation

As in any theory, the results in Myers–Majluf's work are derived under several assumptions. While a vast literature has developed in corporate finance that generalizes many of their assumptions, these papers have two common features: (i) they limit the set of firms to which the theory applies because they invoke *arbitrary* assumptions about one or more firm-specific primitives and (ii) they make limiting assumptions about the "security space." These assumptions have limited our understanding of the impact of *IA* on the firm's financial decisions. We elaborate below:

Firm-Specific Primitives: The existing literature has documented a variety of firm-specific variables that affect the manager's financial decisions. These include the amount of funds the firm requires and, more importantly, the "nature of the manager's private information." The nature of the manager's private information refers to the origin of *IA*. Different firms have *IA* originating from different sources. For example, in some firms the *IA* is about the value of existing assets. This means that the manager knows more about the value of these assets than outside investors. In other firms, the *IA* could be about the value of the firm's new projects. In yet others, it may be about the risk of the firm's projects.

Since the prior research makes specific and arbitrary assumptions about these firm-specific primitives (in particular about nature of the manager's private information), the results of this research do *not* apply to all firms — just to those firms that satisfy those arbitrary assumptions. Some authors [e.g., Frank and Goyal (2005)] have, in fact, noted that this limitation of the theory is a potential explanation for the mixed results of the empirical tests in corporate finance.

To better understand the implications of *IA*, one must thus develop a theory that admits all firms, i.e., relaxes all assumptions regarding these primitives.

The "security space": This is a list of all securities that the manager is assumed to be able to issue when he raises external funds. Since the prior research makes very specific assumptions about the security space, it cannot explain how managers and outside investors will transact when the manager can issue securities not contained in the assumed security space. Nor can it adequately identify the type of financial innovations that can help minimize the inefficiencies arising from *IA*.

I.3. Scope of the Book

Although the prior research has recognized several of the limitations discussed above, it is yet to develop a theory that generalizes the assumptions about the firm-specific primitives and the security space. Accordingly, our book develops a new unifying theoretical framework that examines the manager's financial decisions under *IA* for *any* firm under *any* security space. That is, our theory does not rely on specific assumptions about the firm-specific primitives or about the security space. To isolate the impact of *IA* on the manager's decisions, we ignore other factors that are known to affect these decisions (taxes, bankruptcy costs, agency conflicts, etc.). Further, to simplify matters, we assume that all agents are risk neutral and that *IA* is static.

I.4. Key Contributions

Our unified framework, as we will show, contains existing models as special cases. We also show that our generalization overturns several existing intuitions and yields new theoretical results about: (i) the kind of financing decisions that can minimize *IA*-driven investment inefficiencies, and (ii) how the manager can minimize the *IA*-driven inefficiencies through operational decisions and financing innovation. These new results, as we discuss, help explain many empirical anomalies documented in the literature.

Part II

Basic Setup

II.1. Overview

In our analysis, we have one-period with two-dates, $t = 0$ (t_0) and $t = 1$ (t_1). Here, t_0 represents the present and t_1 the future. Further, we have two economic entities: (i) a firm that has current investors and insufficient capital to invest in projects and (ii) outside investors who are willing to provide the firm capital. In return for this capital, outside investors are issued securities which promise them a share of the firm's future cash flows. All market participants (current and outside investors) have limited liability and thus the most that they can lose is the value of their investment. Further, they are all risk-neutral. The risk-free interest rate is r_f.

In this part, we provide additional details regarding these economic entities and the process by which the firm interacts with the outside investors to raise capital. Chapter 1 focuses on the firm and its need for outside capital. Chapter 2 focuses on outside investors and the securities that they can be issued. Chapter 3 first describes the process by which these two entities interact and raise/supply capital, with a focus on specific decisions that the outside investors and the manager need to make.

It then describes how these decisions yield implications for the firm's financing and investment policies and its "cost (benefit) of raising capital." Here, the cost (benefit) of raising capital is the reduction (increase) in the stockholders' wealth when the firm raises external capital.

Chapter 1

Firm and Its Capital Needs

1.1. Firm

At t_0, the firm is unlevered and has one or more shareholders.[1]
The firm is being run by a manager whose goal is to maximize
the wealth of current (i.e., t_0) shareholders.

The firm has two kinds of assets: (i) assets-in-place, which
consists of fixed assets, FA, and internal capital (cash), L and
(ii) an indivisible investment opportunity (project) that requires
an investment, I.

The fixed assets and the investment opportunity generate
free cash flows at t_1. Free cash flows are the cash flows the firm
generates, net of all expenses. These are also the cash flows that
are available to be distributed to the firm's investors — both

---

[1]This means that, at present, the current shareholders are the only
claimants on the future cash flows generated by the firm. Our analysis can
accommodate a firm that has other claimants, e.g., debt-holders. However,
this complicates the exposition without yielding new insights.

current stockholders and any new outside investors. In the rest of the book, we will refer to free cash flows as simply "cash flows."

The t_1 cash flows from the fixed assets and the project depend on two sets of factors. The first set includes *firm-specific* factors such as business strategy and managerial ability, which are collectively captured by the firm's type, q. Consistent with the existing literature, we assume the firm's type remains constant throughout the period. Further, for simplicity, we assume that the firm is only one of two types; it is either a higher-valued firm ($q = h$) or a lower-valued firm ($q = l$).[2] In the rest of the book, we will use "firm q" ($q = h$ or l) to refer to the firm when it is of type q and "both firm-types" to refer to the firm, regardless of whether it is h and l.

The second set of factors affecting the t_1 cash flows are industry/economy-wide *macro* factors such as interest rates, political risks and exchange rates. We capture these *macro* conditions by the state of the world at t_1, ϕ. We place no assumptions on the number of states of the world next period. Further, we do not assume that all macro factors affect each firm-type identically; some macro factors may affect h more than l while others affect l more. Yet other macro factors may affect both firm-types in the same way.

In sum, the t_1 cash flows from the fixed assets and the project depends *jointly* on the firm-type q, and the state of the world at t_1, ϕ. We therefore denote the t_1 cash flows of firm-type q in state ϕ from fixed assets as $X_q^\phi(FA)$ and from the project as $X_q^\phi(I)$. Thus, if firm-type q does not invest in the project, its total t_1 cash flows are $X_q^\phi(FA)$, and if it does invest in the project, its total t_1 cash flows are $X_q^\phi(FA) + X_q^\phi(I) \equiv X_q^\phi$.

---

[2]Our key results hold even with multiple firm-types. Additional details are available from the authors upon request.

We refer to X_q^ϕ as the *"cum-project cash flows."* Since all market participants have limited liability, it is reasonable to assume that the firm's t_1 cash flows is non-negative regardless of whether or not the manager invests in the project. This means that both $X_q^\phi = X_q^\phi(FA) + X_q^\phi(I) \geq 0$ and $X_q^\phi(FA) \geq 0$. Note that this assumption does not preclude negative *project* cash flows; they can be negative as long as $X_q^\phi(I) \geq -X_q^\phi(FA)$.

We further denote the distribution of firm q's t_1 cash flows from fixed assets as $\tilde{X}_q(FA)$ and the cash flows from the new project as $\tilde{X}_q(I)$. The cum-project cash flow distribution is thus $\tilde{X}_q(FA) + \tilde{X}_q(I) \equiv \tilde{X}_q$.

Since all market participants are risk neutral, the t_0 present values ("values") of these cash flow distributions are simply their expected values discounted at r_f. We denote the value of firm q's cash flows from the new project as $V_q^X(I)$. This value less the initial investment I is the project-*NPV*, $NPV_q(I)$. Here, we assume that the project-*NPV* is positive, regardless of the firm's type.[3] Further, we denote the value of firm q's cash flows from fixed assets as $V_q^X(FA)$ and the cum-project cash flows as $V_q^X \equiv V_q^X(FA) + V_q^X(I)$. Since h is the higher-valued firm, we assume that the cum-project value of firm h exceeds that of l. That is, $V_h^X > V_l^X$.[4]

1.2. Firm's Need for Capital

The firm's t_1 cash flows, and thus the wealth of current shareholders, depends on whether or not the manager invests in the

---

[3]Our model easily accommodates negative-*NPV* projects but it does not yield significant new insights. For this reason, we do not consider negative-*NPV* projects.

[4]Our model admits the $V_h^X = V_l^X$ case [studied in, e.g., Giammarino and Neave (1982)]. Again, it complicates the exposition without yielding new results. We, therefore, ignore this special case.

project. To invest, he requires I in capital. We assume that $L < I$ and do not allow him to sell off any portion of the firm's fixed assets. This means that the manager — if he wants to invest — *must* fund the investment opportunity by raising external capital.

Chapter 2

Outside Investors and Securities

2.1. Outside Investors

The manager can obtain the necessary external capital by approaching outside investors either directly or through a financial intermediary such as an investment bank. We assume that there are N profit-maximizing outside investors, each with enough capital to meet the firm's financing needs. These investors operate in competitive markets. It is well known that the standard capital-raising model is a Bertrand-type analysis [see Nachman and Noe (1994)]. Thus, the markets are equally competitive when $N = 2$ and when $N > 2$.[1] Therefore, for simplicity, we assume that $N = 2$ throughout this analysis.

---

[1] Hence, the free entry assumption that is needed for competitive equilibrium in Cournot-type models [e.g., Rothschild and Stiglitz (1976)] is not required here.

2.2. Securities that the Investors can receive: "Security Space"

In return for providing capital, the manager issues securities to the outside investors at t_0. These securities entitle the investor to a portion of firm q's cum-project $t = 1$ cash flows, X_q^ϕ.[2] The amount of the cum-project cash flows the investor receives, $X_q^\phi(s, \vec{P_s})$, and its $t = 0$ value, $V^s(\tilde{X}_q, \vec{P_s})$, or simply $V_q^s(\vec{P_s})$, depends on the security, s, that he is issued and on the financing terms associated with the security, $\vec{P_s}$. These financing terms are specified by a vector of parameters, each element of which is p_s.[3]

Consider the following three examples of a security:

- Example 1: Zero-coupon debt $(s = D)$. The terms of a zero-coupon debt security are specified by a single parameter: face value, b. The amount of cash flows the investor receives at $t = 1$ under this security is $X_q^\phi(D, b) = min(X_q^\phi, b)$.
- Example 2: Equity $(s = E)$. The terms under an equity security can again be specified by a single parameter: the fraction of total equity issued to the investor, f. The amount of cash flows the investor receives at $t = 1$ is $X_q^\phi(E, f) = f * X_q^\phi$.
- Example 3: Senior zero-coupon debt and junior equity $(s = DE)$. The terms of this security are specified by a vector of two parameters: b and f. The cash flows the investor receives at

---

[2]The firm's cash flows from existing assets and the project individually do not matter. What matters is the cum-project cash flows, $X_q^\phi = X_q^\phi(FA) + X_q^\phi(I)$. Most *IA* models assume that the firm has no fixed assets so that X_q^ϕ reduces to $X_q^\phi(I)$. Thus, in these models, it is the cash flows from the project that matter.

[3]The cash flows received by the investor under a financial contract, say one with $s = D$ (zero-coupon debt), depend on contractual terms (covenants) other than $(s, \vec{P_s})$. However, such terms have no impact in our single-period world. They are thus not considered.

$t = 1$ is $X_q^\phi[DE, (b, f)] = min(X_q^\phi, b) + f * [X_q^\phi - min(X_q^\phi, b)] = (1 - f) * min(X_q^\phi, b) + f * X_q^\phi.$

For a variety of exogenous reasons, the manager can issue only some securities to outside investors. Some of these reasons are firm-specific [e.g., managerial preferences] while others are non-firm-specific [e.g., regulatory reasons, preference for standard securities].[4] We therefore assume that the security issued must come from an exogenously determined set of securities, which we refer to as the security space, S. Consistent with prior research, we abstract from the firm-specific reasons and assume that S is determined by exogenous non-firm-specific factors.

To preserve generality, we allow for *any* security space, as long as each security in S is "admissible" in the sense that it satisfies the four properties discussed below. This means that S can contain just some admissible securities (e.g., just debt and equity) or it can contain all the admissible securities. That is, S is any subset of the set of admissible securities, S^A.

Property 1 (*Limited Liability*). The investor's $t = 1$ payments in state ϕ, $X_q^\phi(s, \vec{P}_s) \in [0, X_q^\phi]$, and the $t = 0$ value of these payments, $V_q^s(\vec{P}_s) \in [0, V_q^X]$.

Property 2 (*Continuity*). Both $X_q^\phi(s, \vec{P}_s)$ and $V_q^s(\vec{P}_s)$ are continuous in p_s. For every $X_q^\phi(s, \vec{P}_s) \in [0, X_q^\phi]$, there is at least one $\vec{P}_s$. Similarly, for every $V_q^s(\vec{P}_s) \in [0, V_q^X]$, there is at least one $\vec{P}_s$.

---

[4]Investors demand an "uncertainty premium" from the firm for holding a non-standard security [Gale (1992)]. Paying this premium reduces firm value. For this reason, the security space generally consists of only standard securities such as debt and equity. This does not mean that new securities will never be part of the security space. Gale argues that if a new security has the potential to be beneficial to many firms, it can be part of the security space since investors are willing to learn about the new security which, in turn, reduces the uncertainty premium.

Property 3 (*Monotonicity*). If $0 < V_q^s(\vec{P}_s) < V_q^X$, the value of the investors' payments either increases, or decreases, monotonically for each $p_s \in \vec{P}_s$.

Property 4 (*Consistency*). If $V_q^s(\vec{P}_s)$ increases (decreases) in p_s under one cash flow distribution, it does so for all.

Commonly-issued securities (e.g., debt, equity, senior debt-junior equity, convertibles, warrants, call options, and futures) and numerous non-standard securities satisfy these four properties. Property 1 is standard in the security design research [e.g., Harris and Raviv (1989)] because, like us, the literature assumes investors have limited liability. Properties 2–4 constrain the relation between $\vec{P}_s$ and the t_1 investor payment, and the value of these payments. Under Property 2, the capital that investors provide under any admissible security is limited only by the value of firm's cash flows. This ensures that the results are not driven by exogenous restrictions on the value of payments the investor can receive from issuing a particular security. With Property 3, only securities for which there is a one-to-one mapping between p_s and $V_q^s(\vec{P}_s)$ are admissible.[5] Property 4 allows for security issuance in a world of incomplete contracting (see Box 1).

Box 1. An Example to Illustrate the Significance of Property 4 (Consistency)

An example illustrates why a security violating Property 4 cannot be rationally priced when there is incomplete contracting. Consider a binomial world (equi-probable states) in which the manager can decide, *ex post*, the firm's cash flow distribution. Assume a zero risk-free rate. There are two scenarios

---

(Continued)

---

[5]Note that this restriction is about p_s, and not $\vec{P}_s$. When $\vec{P}_s$ contains two or more p_s, more than one $\vec{P}_s$ can have the same value of payments.

Box 1. (*Continued*)

that the manager can choose from. In Scenario A, the firm has cash flows of $100 and $50 in the two states, and in Scenario B they are $99 and $51. Now consider an investor that provides the firm $60 in funds today. What should the financing terms be? The answer depends on the security associated with the contract. Consider a security that is described by just one element, p_s. Assume that this security violates Property 4: The value of the investor's cash flows is increasing in p_s under Scenario A, and is decreasing under Scenario B. Further assume that the investor's profits are non-negative, under Scenario A, for $p_s = 17$ and higher and, under Scenario B, for a p_s of 2 or lower (these values are set arbitrarily to illustrate the idea; the example holds as long as p_s under Scenario B is lower than under Scenario A). The investor cannot price-protect himself in this example. If the investor offers a security with $p_s = 17$ or higher, the manager will choose Scenario B. If he offers a security with $p_s = 2$ or lower, the manager will opt for Scenario A. These decisions are optimal because, under these distributions, the manager lowers the value of the firm's obligations to the investor. Further, in both situations, the investor earns negative profits and the firm earns positive profits from financing.

This problem does not arise with securities (like debt) where Property 4 holds. To see why, suppose the investor provided the firm $60 of debt. The investor's profits are non-negative for a face value $b = \$70$ or higher under Scenario A, and for a face value $b = \$69$ or higher under Scenario B. If the investor offers debt with a face value $b = \$70$ he can obtain his required return irrespective of whether the manager chooses Scenario A or B.

Chapter 3

Raising Capital

3.1. Process of Raising Capital

As noted, the manager must raise funds from outside investors if he is to invest in the project. The minimum amount of funds he must raise is $I - L \equiv M$. To raise this capital, the manager approaches both investors *simultaneously* for funds.[1]

3.1.1. *Decisions Investors Need to Make*

When approached, each investor must first decide whether or not he wants to provide capital to the manager by offering him a "financing contract." A financing contract C is described by $[A, s, \vec{P_s}]$ where A denotes the amount of funds the investor provides the manager at t_0 and s is the security that investors receive in return with financing terms $\vec{P_s}$. Each offered security must belong to the security space, i.e., $s \in S$. If an investor decides to provide capital, he must then determine how many

---

[1]Simultaneously does not imply that the manager approaches the two investors at the same time. It simply means that one investor does not know what the other investor has offered the manager.

(one or more) contracts he wants to offer and the $[A, s, \vec{P_s}]$ associated with each offered contract.

Collectively, an investor's decisions can be simply put as follows: His goal is to identify the set of contracts (we call this the "contracts set") that maximizes his expected profits. If he chooses not to provide the firm any capital, the contracts set is a null set and his expected profits are zero.

3.1.2. *Decisions That the Manager Must Make*

When offered these contracts by investors, the manager must make two interrelated decisions. He must first decide whether or not he should accept any of the offered contracts. Of course, if he does not accept an offered contract, he cannot invest in the project. In this situation, he pays out the cash, L, as dividends (since investing in a risk-free asset is not beneficial for shareholders).

If he decides to accept a contract, he must identify the specific offered contract that he should accept. That is, he should identify the contract $C = [A, s, \vec{P_s}]$ that he will accept. We assume that the manager can pick only one contract and, since there are no agency conflicts, he must invest in the project if he accepts a contract.[2] This assumption implies that $A \geq M$ for the chosen contract. Further, if the chosen contract provides funds in excess of what is needed for investment (i.e., $A > M$), the manager pays out the excess to the shareholders (as noted, investing in a risk-free asset is not beneficial for shareholders; it is sub-optimal if the firm chooses a debt contract). It does not

---

[2]Our results hold even when the manager can pick multiple contracts (from multiple investors or the same investor) as long as: (i) all contracts are offered simultaneously, (ii) contract seniority is well defined *a priori* (i.e., each offered contract specifies which other senior contract can be accepted), and (iii) total capital raised is at least M.

matter if the payout is in the form of dividends or repurchases since the manager's goal is to maximize the value of all current stockholders' holdings (not just of those choosing to not tender their shares). Therefore, we assume that the firm's payouts are in the form of cash dividends.[3]

3.1.3. *Importance of Identifying these Decisions*

Clearly, the decisions made by the investor affect the manager's (two) decisions. These managerial decisions, in turn, help identify the firm's investment and financing policies and the cost/benefit associated with raising external finance. The manager's first decision — whether or not to raise external capital — determines the firm's investment policy. Specifically, the firm invests *if and only if* he raises external capital. If he does decide to invest, his second decision — the contract choice — determines the firm's financing policy (and thus also the capital structure) and the cost/benefit of raising capital. Specifically: (i) the firm's financing policy is determined by the $(s, \vec{P}_s)$ of the manager's chosen contract and (ii) cost/benefit of raising capital depends on the amount of capital raised by the firm (inflow) and the value of payments made to the investor (outflow) under the chosen contract.[4]

---

[3]The *IA* literature has modeled equity repurchases in situations where the manager has an incentive to maximize the holdings of those shareholders that do not tender their shares. For example, equity repurchases are significant in Constantinides and Grundy (1989) because the manager, by assumption, maximizes the value of *his* (personal) stock holdings in the firm and, does not tender his shares.

[4]The manager's contract choices also determines two important elements of dividend policy — how much dividend is paid and how the dividend is financed. Specifically, A determines the amount of dividends paid $(A - M)$, and s determines how the dividends are financed. However, we do not discuss the firm's dividend policies when the firm does invest because these

3.2. Organization of Remainder of Book

In order to identify a cash-constrained firm's policies and its cost of raising capital, we must first identify the investors' and the manager's decisions. It is well known that the decisions made by the investors and the manager depend on the assumed frictions in the securities markets — the markets in which the manager and the outside investors transact.

In this book, we examine the manager's capital-raising decisions in security markets when there is IA between the manager and outside investors at t_0 about the t_1 cash flows generated by the fixed assets and the project. To do so, we first examine, in Part III (Chapters 4 and 5), the decisions when the manager and investors have the same information (symmetric information). Then, in Part IV (Chapters 6–11), we introduce IA and examine how the results change. To isolate the impact of IA, we assume, throughout the book that there are no other frictions in the markets (no taxes, no bankruptcy costs, no agency conflicts, no transaction costs, etc.) that is, IA is the only friction.

The proofs for the results developed in the remainder of the book are relegated to the Appendix in Part V.

---

policies are "hard-wired" since the manager, by assumption, pays out all funds not used for investment purposes. To fully analyze a firm's dividend policies, a multi-period model is required; however, such a model is outside the scope of this research. We do not discuss the firm's financing policies when the firm does not invest because these policies are also hard-wired into the model. Specifically, if the firm does not invest (i) it retains its existing capital structure, which by assumption, is all-equity and (ii) it pays L as dividends by assumption.

Part III

Raising Capital When there is Symmetric Information

III.1. Overview

In this part, we examine the manager's capital-raising decisions and the implications of these decisions on the firm's investment and financing policies and on the cost of raising capital in a world of perfect markets with symmetric information. This part consists of two chapters.

Chapter 4 first describes the information possessed by the manager and outside investors. It then focuses on aspects related to decision-making with symmetric information. Specifically, it identifies: (i) the *process* by which the manager and investors make their optimal decisions (not the actual decisions) when capital is being raised and (ii) the primitives affecting these decisions.

Using the process outlined in Chapter 4, Chapter 5 first identifies the optimal decisions of the outside investors and the manager when capital is raised. It then identifies the implications of these decisions on firm policies and demonstrates that the traditional perfect markets finance results obtain. We conclude the chapter with a discussion of factors affecting the firm's policies and the cost of raising capital (Chapter 4 discusses the factors affecting the manager's and investors' decisions).

Chapter 4

Information and Decision-Making with Symmetric Information

4.1. Information Possessed by Manager and Outside Investors

The following describes the information about the future (i.e., t_1) cash flows possessed by the manager/outside investors.

4.1.1. *Information About t_1 Cash Flows at t_0*

As seen, the firm's cash flows depend on the type of the firm, q, and the state of the world at t_1, ϕ. At t_0 both the manager and the outside investors know the firm's type. However, neither knows the state of the world next period; they only know the various possible states that can occur in the future and π^ϕ, the probability of each state occurring.

In sum, both the manager and outside investors at t_0 know the type of the firm and the distributions of cash flows of the firm-type. Since the distributions are known and since all future cash flows are discounted at a known risk-free rate of r_f, it follows that the manager and investors also know, at t_0, the values of these payoff distributions.

4.1.2. *Information About t_1 Cash Flows at t_1*

At t_1, the state of the world, ϕ, is revealed to both the manager and the outside investors. They will thus know the fixed asset cash flows, $X_q^\phi(FA)$, the project cash flows, $X_q^\phi(I)$, and the cum-project cash flows, X_q^ϕ.

4.2. How the Manager and the Investors Make Optimal Decisions

We next identify the process by which the manager and outside investors make their optimal decisions. Since the outside investors and the manager move sequentially, the investors (the first mover) make their optimal decisions by identifying how the actions of the manager (second mover) will be affected by their own choices (the contracts that they may offer). We therefore, first discuss how the manager makes his optimal decisions when offered a set of contract by each investor.

4.2.1. *Manager's Optimal Decisions*

As noted, the manager must make two financing decisions: Whether or not to accept a contract and, if yes, which contract to accept. Also, as seen, the manager knows the firm-type, q (but not the state of the world), and his goal is to make financing decisions that maximize the wealth of current shareholders' t_0 wealth, W_q.

To see how he accomplishes this goal consider, first, the wealth implications of the manager's decision to refuse all contacts. In this case, he receives no new funds, and cannot take on the project. Further, the firm remains all-equity, and the current stockholders receive the current (t_0) and the future (t_1) cash flows in their entirety. The firm's current cash flows are simply the existing cash, L. The future cash flows are the cash flows from the fixed assets, $X_q^\phi(FA)$, and their t_0 value is $V_q^X(FA)$. Thus, W_q is now

$$W_q = L + V_q^X(FA). \qquad (1)$$

Now, consider the situation where the manager accepts a contract $C = [A, s, \vec{P_s}]$ and raises A in external funds. He invests M in the project and, as noted, pays off any remaining funds $A - M = A - (I - L)$ as a t_0 dividend to the current stock holders. Further, the firm's total t_1 cash flows are its cum-project cash flows, X_q^ϕ. Of this amount, $X_q^\phi(s, \vec{P_s})$ is paid to the outside investor in return for the funds provided. The remaining cash flows, $X_q^\phi - X_q^\phi(s, \vec{P_s})$ are paid to the current stockholders as t_1 dividends. The t_0 value of these dividends is $V_q^X - V_q^s(\vec{P_s}) = V_q^X(FA) + V_q^X(I) - V_q^s(\vec{P_s})$. Thus, W_q is now:

$$W_q = A - (I - L) + V_q^X(FA) + V_q^X(I) - V_q^s(\vec{P_s}). \qquad (2)$$

Rewriting this equation yields:

$$W_q = L + V_q^X(FA) + NPV_q(I) + NPV_q^C(F), \qquad (3)$$

where

$$NPV_q(I) \equiv V_q^X(I) - I, \qquad (4)$$
$$NPV_q^C(F) = A - V^s(\tilde{X}_q, \vec{P_s}). \qquad (5)$$

Here, $NPV_q^C(F)$ is firm q's financing-NPV under contract C, which is the t_0 cash received by the firm less the t_1 value of payments made by the firm to the investor under C. $NPV_q^C(F)$ also determines the cost/benefit of raising capital. When $NPV_q^C(F) > 0$, the firm receives more capital than the value of the payments it makes. As a consequence, current stockholders gain from financing. Similarly, when $NPV_q^C(F) < 0$, stockholders lose (there is a cost of raising capital) and when $NPV_q^C(F) = 0$, they neither gain nor lose.

Using Eqs. (1) and (3), we can determine how the manager makes his optimal decisions. Note that the stockholder wealth in (3) is higher than that in (1) *if and only if* $NPV_q(I) + NPV_q^C(F) > 0$. This means that the manager raises external capital and invests in the project *iff* he is offered at least one "economically viable" contract, i.e., one for which $NPV_q^C(F) > -NPV_q(I)$.[1] If he does decide to invest, the stockholders' wealth in (3) is maximized when the manager picks the offered contract with the highest $NPV_q^C(F)$. Taken together, the previous two statements imply that, $NPV_q^C(F)$ for each of the offered contracts is the key variable in determining the manager's optimal choices. Further, in order to make his two inter-related financing decisions, the manager will follow the three steps described below:

Step 1: The manager analyzes each contract offered by the two investors[2] and isolates all economically viable offered contracts, i.e., those for which $NPV_q^C(F) > -NPV_q(I)$.

Step 2: If no contract is economically viable, he rejects all contracts and abandons the project.

Step 3: If at least one contract is viable, he accepts a contract and invests in the project. The contract he accepts is the one that maximizes his firm-type's $NPV_q^C(F)$. If multiple contracts maximize the $NPV_q^C(F)$, and/or multiple investors offer the contract with the highest $NPV_q^C(F)$, he picks both a contract and an investor randomly.

---

[1] For simplicity we assume that the manager does not accept the project if the net impact of raising external financing and investing in the project adds zero wealth, i.e., if $NPV_q(I) + NPV_q^C(F) = 0$.

[2] Recall that we have restricted the number of investors to two only to simplify exposition.

4.2.2. *Investors' Optimal Contracts Set*

Each investor offers a contracts set that maximizes his expected profit. Label this contracts set as Ω^*.

To see how an investor identifies Ω^* note, first, that the investor's expected profit, E^C, from offering a contract, C, depends on: (a) the likelihood that the manager of firm q chooses *his* contract (and not the other investor's), π_q^C and (b) his profits conditional on the manager of firm q choosing his contract. Since financing is a zero-sum transaction, the latter is $-NPV_q^C(F)$ [if the firm gains from financing, the investor loses and vice versa]. Thus,

$$E^C = \pi_q^C[-NPV_q^C(F)]. \tag{6a}$$

This means that an investor's expected profit, E^Ω, from offering contracts set Ω is:

$$E^\Omega = \sum_C \pi_q^C[-NPV_q^C(F)]. \tag{6b}$$

The preceding discussion has three important implications. First, the expected profit earned by an investor depends on the actions of the manager through π_q^C, the probability that the manager will pick his offered contract.

Second, $NPV_q^C(F)$ is the key variable affecting the investor's expected profit, E^C, from offering a contract. This variable has a dual role. The larger the $NPV_q^C(F)$ is, the greater is the likelihood, π_q^C, that the manager chooses this contract offered by the investor (and not any other contract offered by this or another investor). However, the larger the $NPV_q^C(F)$ is, the lower is the investor's profit if his contract is accepted. As will be seen later, understanding this dual role of financing-NPV is critical for identifying the investors' optimal decisions.

Third, the likelihood that the manager will pick a particular investor's contract, π_q^C, will reduce (increase) if the other investor offers contracts with high (low) $NPV_q^C(F)$. Thus, the investor's expected profit depends on the contracts offered by the other investor and the problem of determining each investor's offered contracts set is a game.

We assume that each investor is a Nash-type competitor and can pursue only pure game strategies. In such a game, each investor determines his optimal contracts set, Ω^*, as follows:

Step 1: He starts with any random contracts set, Ω.

Step 2: Using Eq. (6b), he identifies the other investor's "best response contracts set". This is the set of contracts that maximizes the other investor's expected profit given that the first investor offers Ω.

Step 3: Using Eq. (6b), he identifies his profits under Ω assuming that the other investor offers the best response contracts set.

Step 4: He repeats Steps 2–3 for every possible contracts set that he can offer (including the null set, which happens when he does not provide any capital to the firm).

Step 5: He identifies the contracts set Ω that maximizes his expected profit in Step 3 and offers this set. If multiple contracts sets maximize his expected profit, the investor offers the largest set with non-redundant contracts. A redundant contract is one that has a zero probability of being accepted by the manager because it either is not competitive (provides a lower financing-NPV than other offered contracts), or is economically non-viable, or provides $A < M$.[3]

---

[3]In our model, investors determine their contracts set the same way insurers determine their optimal contract in the seminal Rothschild and Stiglitz (1976) analysis.

4.3. Primitives Affecting the Manager's and Investors' Decisions

It follows from the preceding discussion that the manager's and the investors' decisions depend on three primitives. The first two are firm-related factors while the last is not firm-specific:

(i) The firm's financing needs, M. This defines the contracts that do not provide sufficient capital. Such contracts are redundant and will not be offered by investors.

(ii) The cum-project cash flows, X_q^ϕ for each firm-type. This primitive determines each contract's financing-NPV [see Eq. (5)]. This in turn, determines three outcomes: whether or not a contract is economically viable, the current stock-holders' wealth if the manager accepts a contract, and the investor's expected profit from offering the contract.

(iii) The security space, S. Since the manager can only issue securities that are included in S, investors cannot offer contracts containing securities that are not contained in the security space. Thus, S determines the "contracting space" — the set of potential contracts that an investor can offer (and thus the contracts that the manager can accept).

Chapter 5

Optimal Capital-Raising Decisions and their Implications for Firm Policies

5.1. Optimal Decisions

In this chapter, we first identify the outside investors' and the manager's optimal decisions.

The investors' and manager's choices are interrelated and must be determined simultaneously. It is easy to see why. The manager can only pick the contracts offered by the investors and the investors' expected profits from offering a contracts set depend on the manager's decisions [see discussion after Eq. (6)].

We accomplish the goal of simultaneously determining the investors' and manager's choices using the processes described in the previous chapter. The following proposition provides the result.

Proposition 1 (*Optimal Decisions*). Each investor offers firm q all contracts with (i) $s \in S$, (ii) $A \geq M$, and (iii) NPV_q^C

$(F) = 0$. The manager randomly accepts any one of the offered contracts.

Proof. See Appendix.

The intuition behind the result is as follows. The only securities that the investor will be offered are those in the security space, S. Additionally, if the manager is to accept a contract and invest in the project, $A \geq M$; contracts with $A < M$ will not be offered because they will be redundant contracts. Further, the $NPV_q^C(F)$ of the offered contracts is zero because offering other contracts would either lead to investor losses or would not be competitive. To see this point more clearly, suppose that an investor offers a $NPV_q^C(F) > 0$ contract and the firm accepts this contract. Under this contract, the amount of capital that the investor provides to the firm exceeds the value of payments that the investor receives. The investor will therefore lose if he offered this contract. Now suppose that an investor offers a $NPV_q^C(F) < 0$ contract. The firm will not accept this contract because the manager, in competitive markets, can get a contract with higher, albeit non-positive, $NPV_q^C(F)$. In sum, the investors will only offer $NPV_q^C(F) = 0$ contracts.

Finally, because these offered contracts are economically viable [i.e., have $NPV_q^C(F) > -NPV_q(I)$], the manager will raise external financing and invest in the project. And, since each offered contract has the same $NPV_q^C(F)$, the manager will randomly pick any one of the offered contracts.

5.2. Implications for Firm Policies and the Cost of Raising Capital

Having identifying the decisions of the two agents, we next examine the implications of these decisions for the firm's investment and financing policies and the cost/benefit of raising capital.

We begin by focusing on the firm's investment policy. Recall from Chapter 3 that, investment policy depends on whether or not the manager raises external capital. From Proposition 1, firms will raise external capital and invest. Thus, the need for external financing does not lead to the rejection of $NPV_q(I) > 0$ projects, i.e., external financing does not result in under-investment (as under the Fisher Separation Theorem).

We next discuss the cost of raising capital and financing policy. When the manager raises external capital, there is no cost/benefit of raising capital since the financing-NPV of any accepted contract is zero.

The firm's financing policy depends on the $[s, \vec{P_s}]$ of the chosen contract. The investor offers the firm-type all $NPV_q^C(F) = 0$ contracts with $A \geq M$ and the manager picks any $NPV_q^C(F) = 0$ contract. Thus, to identify the firm's financing policy, it is necessary to determine the $[s, \vec{P_s}]$ of all the $NPV_q^C(F) = 0$ contracts. Since all securities in S are admissible, it is straightforward to show that:

Proposition 2 (*Financing Policy*). The firm's financing policy is "completely irrelevant" in the sense that the firm can have any capital structure after it raises capital.

Proof. See Appendix.

5.3. Primitives Affecting Firm Policies and the Cost of Raising Capital

As seen, the security space and the two firm-specific primitives, $[M, X_q^\phi]$ affect the investors' and manager's decisions in the sense that they determine the terms of the contracts offered and accepted. However, none of our primitives affect the firm's investment and financing policies and the cost of raising capital. Regardless of S and $[M, X_q^\phi]$, the firm's cost of raising capital will be zero, the Fisher Separation Theorem holds, and financing policy is irrelevant. All of these symmetric information results are well known.

Thus, taken collectively, our analysis in this chapter shows that we obtain the standard results in a world of symmetric information.

Part IV

Raising Capital with Information Asymmetry

In this part, we introduce information asymmetry (IA) between the manager and outside investors and examine the outside investors' and manager's capital-raising decisions and the implications of these decisions for firm's investment and financing policies and cost of raising capital.

This part consists of six chapters.

Chapter 6 first describes the information possessed by the manager and outside investors. It then describes the process by which these agents make their optimal decisions when capital is being raised. It finally shows that the firm's capital needs, the nature of the manager's private information, and the security space are the economic primitives affecting these decisions. The first two primitives are firm-specific while the last (the security space) is not.

It is useful to restate here that what separates our analysis from the prior research is that we place no assumptions on the firm-specific primitives and rely on only very parsimonious assumptions on the security space. Thus, our analysis applies to any firm under any security space. To discuss the results of our generalized framework in a more comprehensible manner, we break down our analysis into four chapters.

In Chapter 7, we first determine the manager's and the investors' optimal decisions under any security space, S. We then examine the implications of these decisions for the firm's investment and financing policies and the cost of raising capital. We next discuss the primitives affecting these policies and the cost of raising capital. We conclude with a discussion of how the implications of Chapter 7, while very important, are too general to derive empirical predictions and implications useful to practitioners. To obtain more specific implications, one must apply the general model to *specific* security spaces.

Chapters 8 derives these additional implications for a particular security space: The debt and equity security space. The same process can be used to determine these implications for *any* other security space. We focus on the debt and equity security space since a majority of firms issue, for exogenous reasons, only these two securities and further, a preponderance of the empirical corporate finance research focuses on a firm's debt-equity choice.

Chapter 9 illustrates, with numerical examples, the key financing policy results derived in Chapter 8 for the debt-equity security space.

Chapter 10 discusses the empirical predictions of the findings in Chapter 8 and some implications for practitioners. We first focus on implications related to financing policy. We then discuss the implications regarding investment policy. We finally discuss how the markets will react to the firm's financing and investment choices.

Chapter 11 concludes with some suggestions for future research.

Chapter 6

Information and Decision-Making with Information Asymmetry

6.1. Information Possessed by the Manager and Outside Investors

At t_0, the manager knows whether the firm is a higher-valued firm $(q = h)$ or a lower-valued firm $(q = l)$; however outside investors do not. They only know that there is a probability π_q that the firm is of type-q. This means that the manager at t_0 knows whether the distribution of the firm's t_1 cash flows is $\tilde{X}_h$ or $\tilde{X}_l$. However, outside investors only know that the distribution of these cash flows is drawn from $\theta^x = (\tilde{X}_h, \tilde{X}_l)$ with probabilities (π_h, π_l).

Thus, at t_0, there is IA in the sense that the manager possesses (private) information about the distribution of the firm's t_1 cash flows that outside investors do not have.[1] Further, θ^x can be thought of as the nature of the manager's private information.

---

[1]In some models [e.g., Axelson (2007)] investors have private information that the manager does not.

For example, suppose θ^x is such that $X_h^\phi = \mu_h - \varepsilon^\phi$ and $X_l^\phi = \mu_l - \varepsilon^\phi$ where $\sum_\phi \varepsilon^\phi = 0$ and $\mu_h > \mu_l$. Here, the manager has private information about the mean of cash flows; the manager and outside investors have the same information about all other moments of the cash flow distribution.

To see why this is the case, first note that the macro conditions affect the two firm-types identically. As a result, $\tilde{X}_h$ is greater than $\tilde{X}_l$ by the same amount in each state of the world. This means that the two firm-types will have different means but they will have the same values for all the other moments of the cash flow distributions (such as variance, skewness, etc.). Consequently the manager, who knows the firm-type but not the state of the world, has private information only about the mean of the cash flows.

While the manager has private information about the firm's t_1 cash flow distributions at t_0, this private information disappears at t_1. As in symmetric information (Chapter 4), we assume that at t_1, both the manager and outside investors know the firm-type, q, and the state of the world, ϕ. Thus, at t_1, both will know the fixed asset cash flows, $X_q^\phi(FA)$, the project cash flows, $X_q^\phi(I)$, and the cum-project cash flows, X_q^ϕ.

6.2. How the Manager and the Investors Make Optimal Decisions

As in the symmetric information case, here too the manager knows the firm-type and thus knows the true cash flow distribution. Therefore, to make his optimal decisions the manager follows the same steps that were outlined following Eq. (5) in Chapter 4. Specifically, the manager identifies all economically viable contracts [i.e., those for which $NPV_q^C(F) > -NPV_q(I)$] and picks the one that maximizes his firm-type's $NPV_q^C(F)$.

The goal of the outside investor remains the same as in the symmetric information case: offer the contracts set, Ω^*, that maximizes expected profits. However, an investor's profit from offering a contract is not the same as Eq. (6a) in Chapter 4. This is because he no longer knows the firm-type.

To determine the investor's expected profit, we first determine, $E^C|h$, his profit conditional on the firm being of type-h. From (6a), we know that this will be:

$$E^C|h = \pi_h^C \left[-NPV_h^C(F)\right]. \tag{7a}$$

Similarly, his profit conditional on the firm being of type l is:

$$E^C|l = \pi_l^C[-NPV_l^C(F)]. \tag{7b}$$

While the investor does not know the firm-type, he does know that the firm is of type h will a probability of π_h and of type l with a probability of π_l. Thus, his expected (unconditional) profit from offering a contract, C, is:

$$E^C = \pi_h\pi_h^C[-NPV_h^C(F)] + \pi_l\pi_l^C[-NPV_l^C(F)] \tag{7c}$$

and his profit from offering a contracts set, Ω is:

$$E^\Omega = \sum_C \pi_h\pi_h^C[-NPV_h^C(F)] + \pi_l\pi_l^C[-NPV_l^C(F)]. \tag{7d}$$

The discussion above yields four important implications. First, each investor's expected profit depends on what the manager's actions would be if his firm is of type h *and* if it is firm type l.

Second, as in the symmetric information case, $NPV_q^C(F)$ is the key variable affecting the investor's expected profit, E^C, from offering a contract. And, as before, this variable has a dual role. The larger (smaller) the $NPV_q^C(F)$, the greater (lower) is the chance that the manager of firm q will accept his offered contract and the lower (greater) is the investor's profit if his contract is accepted. However, unlike under symmetric information, the investor must now consider $NPV_q^C(F)$ of both firm-types.

Third, the nature of the manager's private information, $\theta^x \equiv (X_h^\phi, X_l^\phi)$, determines the investor's expected profits when he offers any contracts set, Ω. This is because the investors' profits depend on the $NPV_q^C(F)$ of both firm-types, which, in turn, depend on X_q^ϕ for both firm-types. For this reason, θ^x can affect the investor's optimal set Ω^*. Thus, alternative assumptions about θ^x will alter the decisions made by the investor, and hence the firm's policies and cost of raising capital.

Fourth, the likelihood that the manager of firm q will pick a particular investor's contract reduces (increases) if the other investors offer contracts with high (low) $NPV_q^C(F)$. Thus, as under symmetric information, the investor's expected profit depends on the contracts offered by the other investor. Hence, the problem of determining each investor's offered contracts set is still a game. The steps that the investor will follow in determining his optimal contracts set are the same as in Chapter 4 except that he will now use Eq. (7d) to determine his expected profits [instead of Eq. (6b)].

6.3. Primitives Affecting the Manager's and Investors' Decisions

In symmetric information, the optimal decisions depend on three primitives: One non-firm-specific primitive, S, and two firm-specific primitives, the firm's financing needs and its cum-project t_1 cash flows.

The analysis above demonstrates that in a world of IA, the investor and manager use the same process as under symmetric information to determine their optimal decisions, albeit with an important distinction: investors, since they do not know q, must consider both firm-types. This means that the same three primitives affect optimal decisions, but the investor must consider X_q^ϕ for each firm-type [S and M are independent of firm-type]. In other words, the optimal decisions depend on one non-firm-specific primitive, S and two firm-specific primitives: $[M, (X_h^\phi X_l^\phi) \equiv \theta^x]$. Recall that θ^x also measures the nature of the manager's private information.

Since we place only parsimonious assumptions regarding the security space, S and make no assumptions about the firm-specific primitives, our analysis admits essentially all firms and all security spaces. Given the generality of our framework, our analysis is fairly long. We, therefore, spread the discussion over the next four chapters.

Chapter 7

Optimal Capital-Raising Decisions and their Implications: Any Security Space

7.1. Optimal Decisions

We first identify the optimal decisions of the investors and the manager (of both firm-types). The manager's decisions depend on the investors' offered contracts, which, in turn, depend on the manager's potential choices. The rationale is similar to that in the symmetric information case (examined in Chapter 5). Further, since an investor does not know the firm's type, he must consider the manager's potential decisions for both firm-types.

The previous discussion means that the investors' choices and the two firm-types' manager's choices must be determined simultaneously.

We accomplish this goal in three steps. In each step, the key variable in our analysis is $NPV_q^C(F)\forall q$. This is because, as discussed, $NPV_q^C(F)$ affects both the stockholders' wealth and the investors' expected profits. Further, since the investor does not know the firm-type, he must consider the $NPV_q^C(F)$ for both firm-types.

7.1.1. *Step 1: Pooled and No-loss Contracts*

There are potentially an infinite number of contracts that an investor can offer and the manager can accept. In the first step, we simplify the problem by introducing the notions of "pooled" and "no-loss" contracts and showing that these are the only relevant contracts in a world of information asymmetry (IA).

We begin with the definition of a pooled contract.

Definition: A contract $C \equiv (A, s, \vec{P}_s)$ is a pooled contract *iff* the investors' expected profits, E^C, are zero when both firm-types pick the contract.

Under this definition, a pooled contract is one under which:

$$A = \sum_q \pi_q V^s \left(\tilde{X}_q, \vec{P}_s \right). \qquad (8)$$

To see why, recall that if both firm-types pick the contract (i.e., $\pi_h^C = \pi_l^C = 1$), then from Eq. (7c), the investor's expected profits are

$$E^C = \pi_h \left[-NPV_h^C(F) \right] + \pi_l \left[-NPV_l^C(F) \right]$$

$$= -\sum_q \pi_q NPV_q^C(F). \qquad (9a)$$

Substituting $NPV_q^C(F)$ from Eq. (5) into (9a) yields that:

$$E^C = -\sum_q \pi_q \left[A - V^s(\tilde{X}_q, \vec{P}_s) \right]. \qquad (9b)$$

By definition, a pooled contract is one for which $E^C = 0$. That is, it is a contract for which Eq. (8) is satisfied. The definition of a pooled contract thus implies that it is a contract under which $\left(s, \vec{P}_s\right)$ is such that the probability-weighted average of the values of payments h and l made under the contract is equal to the amount of capital provided under the contract.

Next consider another type of contract, a no-loss contract.

Definition: A no-loss contract $C \equiv \left(A, s, \vec{P}_s\right)$ is one that provides the largest amount of capital, A, while satisfying the requirement that the investors' expected profits, E^C, are non-negative regardless of the firm-type that picks the contract.

Under this definition, a no-loss contract is one that satisfies the following two conditions:

$$A = Min\left[V^s\left(\tilde{X}_h, \vec{P}_s\right), V^s\left(\tilde{X}_l, \vec{P}_s\right)\right]. \tag{10a}$$

$$V^s\left(\tilde{X}_h, \vec{P}_s\right) \neq V^s\left(\tilde{X}_l, \vec{P}_s\right). \tag{10b}$$

To see why, note that if only h picks the contract, then from Eq. (7c), the investor's expected profits are:

$$E^C = \pi_h\left[-NPV_h^C(F)\right]. \tag{11a}$$

Substituting $NPV_h^C(F)$ using Eqs. (5) into (11a) yields that:

$$E^C = \pi_h\left[-\left\{A - V^s\left(\tilde{X}_h, \vec{P}_s\right)\right\}\right]. \tag{11b}$$

Similarly, if only l picks the contract, the investor's expected profits are:

$$E^C = \pi_l * \left[-\left\{A - V^s\left(\tilde{X}_l, \vec{P}_s\right)\right\}\right]. \tag{11c}$$

Equations (11b) and (11c) imply that the investor's profits remain non-negative regardless of whether h or l picks the contract *iff* $A \leq V^s\left(\tilde{X}_h, \vec{P}_s\right)$ and $A \leq V^s\left(\tilde{X}_l, \vec{P}_s\right)$ That is, *iff* $A \leq Min\left[V^s\left(\tilde{X}_h, \vec{P}_s\right), V^s\left(\tilde{X}_l, \vec{P}_s\right)\right]$. Further, by definition, the no-loss contract provides the largest amount of capital such that profits remain non-negative. That is, it must satisfy (10a). Further, for a no-loss contract to be distinct from a pooled contract, the value of payments made by h and l must be different (otherwise, from Eq. (8), it is a pooled contract). That is, it must also satisfy Eq. (10b).

Thus the definition of a no-loss contract implies that it is a contract under which $\left(s, \vec{P_s}\right)$ is such that (i) the minimum value of payments that h and l would make under the contract is equal to the amount of capital provided and (ii) the value of payments made by h and l is different.

Define the "candidate contracts set" as the set of all pooled and no-loss contracts for which $A \geq M$ and $s \in S$. By definition, this set depends on the security space, S, and the firm's financing needs, M. In addition, it is evident from Eqs. (8) and (10a)–(10b) that the amount of capital provided under pooled and no-loss contracts depends on $\left(\tilde{X}_h, \tilde{X}_l\right) \equiv \theta^x$. Thus, the composition of the candidate contracts set also depends on θ^x. We therefore denote this set as $\Omega^C[\theta^x, M, S]$.[1] Consistent with the literature following Rothschild and Stiglitz (1976), we have:

Proposition 3 (*Pooled and No-loss Contracts*). The only contracts that an investor can offer (and a manager can accept) are those in the candidate contracts set, $\Omega^C[\theta^x, M, S]$. This is the set of all pooled and no-loss contracts for which $A \geq M$ and $s \in S$.

Proof. See Appendix.

The intuition behind the result is as follows. With IA, it is well known that there can be two possibilities in equilibrium:

---

[1]Here, the project-NPV does not affect the composition of the candidate contracts set because we have assumed $NPV_q(I) > 0 \forall q$ for both firm-types. Project-NPV matters when it is allowed to be negative. However, as noted earlier, such a generalization yields no new insights.

firm-types either "pool" or "separate." In a pooling equilibrium, both firm-types choose the same contract and, as Rothschild and Stiglitz (1976) have demonstrated, the uninformed party (here, the investor) earns zero economic profits. This implies that, in a pooling equilibrium, only a pooled contract can be chosen. In a separating equilibrium, a contract can be chosen by only one firm-type. Further, no firm-type can gain from financing; otherwise the investors will lose [Rothschild and Stiglitz (1976)]. To ensure that no firm-type gains from financing, such contracts must have $NPV_q^C(F) \leq 0 \forall q$ i.e., if $A \leq Min[V^s(\tilde{X}_h, \vec{P}_s), V^s(\tilde{X}_l, \vec{P}_s)]$. Competitive investors will try to offer financing terms that maximize the stockholders' wealth. From Eq. (5), it is clear that they can maximize stockholders' wealth, regardless of firm-type, by providing the maximum amount of capital, i.e., if $A = Min[V^s(\tilde{X}_h, \vec{P}_s), V^s(\tilde{X}_l, \vec{P}_s)]$. Thus, in a separating equilibrium, only a no-loss contract can be chosen.

7.1.2. *Step 2: Composition of the Candidate Contracts Set*

Proposition 3 implies that the only economically relevant contracts are those in the candidate contracts set. This means that to determine the contracts investors will offer and the ones that the manager can accept, we only need to examine the contracts in $\Omega^C[\theta^x, M, S]$, not the universe of contracts.

We therefore examine, as a second step, the composition of the contracts in $\Omega^C[\theta^x, M, S]$ based on the $NPV_q^C(F) \forall q$ for these contracts.[2] Somewhat surprisingly, we find in Proposition 4

---

[2]We examine the composition based on $NPV_q^C(F) \forall q$ because, as noted several times, the financing-*NPV* of a contract determines whether it will be offered by the investors and accepted by the manager and further, since the investor does not know the firm-type, it is important to examine financing-*NPV*s of the contract for both firm-types.

that, for any firm [i.e., for any $(\theta^x M)$] under any security space, $S \subseteq S^A$, the candidate contracts set can take on any one of just two compositions.

To see this, first consider the $NPV_q^C(F) \forall q$ of pooled contracts in Ω. Substituting A from Eq. (8) into (5) and rewriting using $\pi_h + \pi_l = 1$ shows that:

$$NPV_h^C(F) = -\pi_l \left[V^s(\tilde{X}_h, \vec{P}_s) - V^s(\tilde{X}_l, \vec{P}_s) \right], \qquad (12a)$$

$$NPV_l^C(F) = \pi_h \left[V^s(\tilde{X}_h, \vec{P}_s) - V^s(\tilde{X}_l, \vec{P}_s) \right], \qquad (12b)$$

As Eqs. (12a)–(12b) show, h loses and l gains under a pooled contract when h's payments exceed those made by l. On the other hand, l loses and h gains when l's payments are higher. Both firm-types break even when they make identical payments. By definition, an investor's expected profits are zero if both firm-types accept this contract. However, if only the firm-type that gains (loses) accepts the contract, the investor suffers a loss (profit) and the size of his loss (profit) depends on the difference in payments made by the two firm-types.

Next consider the no-loss contracts. Substituting A from Eqs. (10a)–(10b) into (5) and rewriting shows that:

$$NPV_h^C(F) = min \left[0, -\left(V^s(\tilde{X}_h, \vec{P}_s) - V^s(\tilde{X}_l, \vec{P}_s) \right) \right], \quad (13a)$$

$$NPV_l^C(F) = min \left[0, \left(V^s(\tilde{X}_h, \vec{P}_s) - V^s(\tilde{X}_l, \vec{P}_s) \right) \right], \quad (13b)$$

and

$$NPV_h^C(F) \neq NPV_l^C(F). \qquad (13c)$$

Equations (13a)–(13c) show that, depending upon whether a firm-type makes higher or lower payments, it either loses or is indifferent about accepting a no-loss contract; it can never gain. Specifically, $h(l)$ loses and $l(h)$ breaks even for a no-loss contract when the payments by $h(l)$ are higher.[3] *Ex-ante*, an investor will not lose regardless of whether the firm accepting the contract is h or l; however, he can gain if the firm-type accepting the contract loses.

Collectively, this discussion implies that the financing-NPV of pooled and no-loss contracts in $\Omega^C[\theta^x, M, S]$ depends on the difference in value of payments made by the firm-types, $V^s(\tilde{X}_h, \vec{P}_s) - V^s(\tilde{X}_l, \vec{P}_s)$, under the contract. This difference in value of payments made by the firm-types under a pooled/no-loss contract, clearly depends on the $(s, \vec{P}_s)$ of each contract and on the nature of private information, $(\tilde{X}_h, \tilde{X}_l) \equiv \theta^x$. We therefore denote $V^s(\tilde{X}_h, \vec{P}_s) - V^s(\tilde{X}_l, \vec{P}_s)$ by $R^s(\theta^x, \vec{P}_s)$.

This insight, in conjunction with the facts that $V_h^X > V_l^X$ and each security in S is admissible yields the result that $\Omega^C[\theta^x, M, S]$ can take on one of just two compositions. Under the first potential composition, h loses while l either gains or is indifferent under all contracts. The second composition also includes contracts under which h neither gains nor loses ($NPV_l^C(F) \leq 0$ under these contracts).

Proposition 4 (*Composition of the Candidate Contracts Set*). The candidate contracts set, $\Omega^C[\theta^x, M, S]$, has one of two mutually exclusive, yet exhaustive, compositions for any firm under any security space $S \subseteq S^A$.

(i) Composition 1: The candidate contracts set contains only pooled contracts with $NPV_h^C(F) < 0$ and $NPV_l^C(F) > 0$ and no-loss contracts with $NPV_l^C(F) = 0$ and $NPV_h^C(F) < 0$.

(ii) Composition 2: The candidate contracts set contains a contract with $NPV_h^C(F) = 0$ and $NPV_l^C(F) \leq 0$. In addition, it also contains pooled contracts with $NPV_h^C(F) < 0$ and

---

[3]From (10b), it follows that no-loss contracts where both firm-type make the same payments are not defined.

$NPV_l^C(F) > 0$ and no-loss contracts with $NPV_l^C(F) = 0$ and $NPV_h^C(F) < 0$.

Proof. See Appendix.

7.1.3. *Step 3: Equilibrium Contracts Set and Managerial Choices*

In the final step, we identify the equilibrium contracts set and the manager's choices when offered this set.

In this regard, a brief discussion of Propositions 3 and 4 is useful. First, the only contracts that can *potentially* be offered and accepted are in the candidate contracts set, $\Omega^C[\theta^x, M, S]$. Second, this set can have only one of two compositions.

Together these two findings imply that to determine the equilibrium contracts set and the manager's choices, we must identify the contracts in $\Omega^C[\theta^x, M, S]$ that are offered/accepted under each composition. To do so, we follow the steps outlined after Eqs. (5) and (6).

The next set of propositions provides the results of this analysis. Here, $C_h^{P_{max}}$ is the pooled contract(s) that maximizes h's financing-NPV (i.e., minimizes h's financing cost).

Proposition 5a (*Equilibrium Contracts Set and Manager's Decisions: Composition 1*). If the candidate contracts set, $\Omega^C[\theta^x, M, S]$ contains only $NPV_h^C(F) < 0$ contracts, two situations arise:

(i) The $C_h^{P_{max}}$ contract is economically viable for h: The equilibrium contracts set contains the $C_h^{P_{max}}$ contract and both firm-types accept the contract.

(ii) The $C_h^{P_{max}}$ contract is not viable for h: The equilibrium contracts set contains all no-loss contracts; the manager of firm-type h rejects all contracts. If the firm-type is l, the manager accepts any offered no-loss contract.

Proposition 5b (*Equilibrium Contracts Set and Manager's Decisions: Composition 2*). If $\Omega^C[\theta^x, M, S]$ also contains $NPV_h^C(F) = 0$ contract(s), then

(i) The equilibrium contracts set contains all pooled contracts under which both firm-types break even, and all no-loss contracts.

(ii) The manager of firm h chooses any pooled or no-loss contract with $NPV_h^C(F) = 0 (NPV_l^C(F) \leq 0$ under these contracts). The manager of firm l chooses any pooled or no-loss contract with $NPV_l^C(F) = 0$ ($NPV_h^C(F) \leq 0$ under these contracts).

Proof. See Appendix.

Several aspects of the equilibrium contracts set and managerial decisions are noteworthy. First, the investors' expected profits are, *ex ante*, zero. They cannot earn positive profits because the markets are competitive and because profit-maximizing investors will not offer contracts that yield negative profits. Second, all investors offer the same contracts set. This should not be surprising since each investor has the same information about the firm. Third, there always is an equilibrium; investors can always identify a contracts set to offer. Fourth, the equilibrium is unique: There is *only* one equilibrium contracts set for a given (θ^x, M) and S. With uniqueness, the manager's decisions identified in Propositions 5a and 5b are the *only* decisions that he can make. This imputes greater validity to our findings.

Some additional discussion can be useful for bringing out the relevance of the last two points. There are two solution methodologies with IA — signaling and screening. The key distinction between the two in capital raising games is regarding who first proposes the financing contract. In signaling models, it is the manager (the informed party) who first proposes the financing contracts while in screening models, it is the outside investors (the uninformed party) who propose the financing contracts.

Each model has its potential advantages and disadvantages. In signaling models, there is always at least one equilibrium. However, it is well known that these models can have multiple equilibria depending on how one specifies out-of-equilibrium beliefs; although unique equilibriums can be obtained by invoking restrictions on out-of-equilibrium beliefs [see Nachman and Noe (1994) for a detailed discussion on this matter]. In addition, they "...generally fail to yield empirical predictions beyond the ones for which they were custom tailored" [Brennan (1995, p. 13)]. Also, empirical evidence indicates that few firms have signaling motives when they raise capital [Graham and Harvey (2001, p. 222)].

In contrast, it is well known that screening models do not require specification of out-of-equilibrium beliefs and that they do not yield multiple equilibria. A potential disadvantage of a screening model is that it may not yield an equilibrium at all [e.g., as in the insurance markets analysis of Rothschild and Stiglitz (1976)].

Most capital-raising models use a signaling methodology. In contrast, we are using a screening model — the investors first propose the financing contracts. As seen, the problem of multiple equilibria or of the absence of equilibrium does not arise in our model.[4] This, coupled with the empirical evidence that signaling is not a motive for managers when making financial decisions, would suggest that future research on the firm's capital-raising

---

[4]This finding is consistent with Innes (1993), who also uses a screening methodology with the same basic setup as ours.

decision should first attempt to use screening models as a solution methodology.[5]

7.2. Implications for Firm Policies and the Cost of Raising Capital

The managerial decisions in Propositions 5a–5b identify the implications of raising capital in a world of IA. The implications fall into one of two cases. These are discussed next in detail and also summarized in Table 1.

(1) The first case obtains when firm parameters, (θ^x, M), and the security space, S, are such that $NPV_h^C(F) < 0$ $\left(NPV_l^C(F) \geq 0\right)$ for all contracts in $\Omega^C[\theta^x, M, S]$. The managerial decisions in this case are outlined in Proposition 5a. The decisions vary depending on whether the $C_h^{P_{max}}$ contract is viable for h or not. Consider both possibilities:

(a) $C_h^{P_{max}}$ is not viable for h: In this case the manager of h refuses all contracts, abandons his positive-NPV project, and thus under-invests. On the other hand, l picks any offered no-loss contract and invests in the project. Further, it neither gains nor loses from financing. Finally, as the following Proposition demonstrates, the investors offer l all contracts with $NPV_l^C(F) = 0$.

Proposition 6a (*Irrelevance for l*). Investors offer all $NPV_l^C(F) = 0$ contracts.

Proof. See Appendix.

---

[5]Interestingly, it should be noted that our findings remain unchanged even in a signaling model that includes the restrictions on the out-of-equilibrium beliefs described in Nachman and Noe (1994). Further research regarding the conditions under which screening and signaling models yield identical results might be useful.

Since the manager can accept any one of these contracts, financing policy is completely irrelevant. That is, capital structure is entirely inconsequential.

(b) $C_h^{P_{max}}$ is viable for h: Both h and l choose this contract and accept the project. In this case, since h loses under all pooled contracts, it will also lose under $C_h^{P_{max}}$, even though, by definition, this pooled contract maximizes h's financing-NPV (i.e., minimizes h's loss). With h losing under this pooled contract, l gains. Further, the magnitude of h's loss and l's gain depends on each firm-type's NPV under the $C_h^{P_{max}}$ contract. Finally, financing policy depends on the security issued under the $C_h^{P_{max}}$ contract.

The following proposition regarding pooled contracts is useful for identifying this security. In this proposition, $A^{P_{max}} \equiv \sum_q \pi_q V_q^X$ is the firm's pre-financing firm value.

Proposition 6b (*Pooled Contract Properties*). Irrespective of the security issued with a pooled contract, the graph of $NPV_h^C(F)$ versus A is continuous and has the same beginning and ending points. The graph's beginning point is $A = 0$ and $NPV_h^C(F) = 0$. The end point is $A = A^{P_{max}}$ and $NPV_h^C(F) = -\pi_l(V_h^X - V_l^X)$.

Proof. See Appendix.

Proposition 6b implies that the security in S with the smallest second derivative, $\frac{\partial^2 NPV_h^C(F)}{\partial A^2}$, for all A must be the security issued under the $C_h^{P_{max}}$ contract. Label the security with the smallest second derivative as the "most concave security."[6] It is entirely possible that no one

---

[6]Note that here we are considering the case where the θ^x is such that $NPV_h^C(F) < 0$ for all contracts, i.e., h's financing loss is always positive.

security in S has the smallest second derivative across all A. In other words, the most concave security may not exist. In this case, the security issued with the $C_h^{P_{max}}$ contract depends on A, and thus on the firm's financing needs, M. More formally,

Proposition 6c ($C_h^{P_{max}}$ *Contract Security*). The security associated with the $C_h^{P_{max}}$ contract depends on whether or not a most concave security can be found in S. If such a security exists, then it is the $C_h^{P_{max}}$ contract security. If it does not exist, the $C_h^{P_{max}}$ contract security depends on the firm's financing needs.

(2) The second case obtains when (θ^x, M) and S are such that $\Omega^C[\theta^x, M, S]$ also contains contract(s) under which $NPV_h^C(F) = 0$ [$NPV_l^C(F) \leq 0$ under these contracts]. In this situation, note from Proposition 5b, that both h and l choose an offered contract and accept the project. Also, neither h nor l gains or loses under the chosen contract. Thus, neither firm-type under-invests and there is no financing cost/benefit due to IA.[7] This brings up an immediate question. With costless external financing, is financing policy even relevant? The answer entails some new terminology:

Partial Irrelevance. Financing policies are "partially irrelevant" if a firm's optimal capital structure choice

---

Therefore, the security in S with the smallest $\frac{\partial^2 NPV_h^C(F)}{\partial A^2}$ is also the security with the largest second derivative (with respect to A) of the financing loss. In other words, the most concave security in terms of financing-NPV is the most convex security in terms of financing loss.

[7] The result that IA is costless when $\Omega^C[\theta^x, M, S]$ contains both a contract with $NPV_h^C(F) = 0$ and $NPV_l^C(F) \leq 0$ and a contract with $NPV_l^C(F) = 0$ and $NPV_h^C(F) \leq 0$ is consistent with Heinkel (1982) and Brennan and Kraus (1987).

is flexible, but only within a feasible range of choices. This obtains if investors offer just *some* $NPV_q^C(F) = 0$ contracts.[8]

In the present discussion, investors offer the manager only those $NPV_q^C(F) = 0$ contracts for which financing-*NPV* is non-positive for the other firm-type; they do not offer those $NPV_q^C(F) = 0$ contracts for which financing-*NPV* is positive for the other firm-type. Financing choices are thus partially irrelevant (flexible, but not completely so).

7.3. The Primitives Affecting the Firm's Policies and its Cost of Raising Capital

The following primitives affect firm policies with *IA*:

(1) *Firm's Financing Needs.* The firm's financing needs, M, determines the number of contracts in the candidate contracts set, $\Omega^C[\theta^x, M, S]$. This, in turn, determines: (i) whether *IA* is costly or costless, (ii) the range of financing choices when *IA* is costless, and (iii) financing policy when *IA* is costly and the most concave security does not exist.

A simple example illustrates how M affects item (i). Suppose for a particular M, the candidate contracts set for a firm contains only contracts with $NPV_h^C(F) < 0$. In this case, *IA* is costly (beneficial) to $h(l)$. Now suppose we reduce the financing needs. This increases the number of contracts in the candidate contracts set and, if $NPV_h^C(F) = 0$ under one of the new contracts, *IA* is now costlessly resolved.

---

[8]In contrast, financing policies are completely irrelevant if capital structure is inconsequential (as under symmetric information). As seen, this situation obtains if investors offer firm-type q all $NPV_q^C(F) = 0$ contracts.

Table 1. *IA* Implications for any firm under any S.

I. If the firm parameters, (θ^x, M) and the security space, S, are such that the candidate contracts set, $\Omega^C[\theta^x, M, S]$:	II. Investment policy	III. Financing policy	IV. Financing cost/benefit
Contains only contracts with $NPV_h^C(F) < 0$ [$NPV_l^C(F) \geq 0$ under these contracts] and $C_h^{P_{max}}$ is:			
Economically viable for h	Both firm-types invest in the project	Financing policy depends on the security associated with the $C_h^{P_{max}}$ contract. This security is the most concave security. If the most concave security does not exist, the firm's financing needs, M, determines the security associated with the $C_h^{P_{max}}$ contract	h loses while l gains. Magnitude of h's loss and l's gain depends on NPV of firm-type under the $C_h^{P_{max}}$ contract
Not economically viable for h	Only l invests; h does not (it under-invests)	h: retains existing capital structure l: Completely irrelevant	h: Does not raise external capital l: Breaks even

(*Continued*)

Table 1. (*Continued*)

I. If the firm parameters, (θ^x, M) and the security space, S, are such that the candidate contracts set, $\Omega^C[\theta^x, M, S]$:	II. Investment policy	III. Financing policy	IV. Financing cost/benefit
Also contains contract(s) with $NPV_h^C(F) = 0$ ($NPV_l^C(F) \leq 0$ under these contracts)	Both firm-types invest in the project	Partially irrelevant: Each firm type's capital structure choice is flexible, but only within the feasible range of choices: each firm-type can pick any contract in $\Omega^C[\theta^x, M, S]$ for which $NPV_q^C(F) = 0$ and the financing-NPV is non-positive for the other firm-type	Both firm-types break even

In Table 1, $C_h^{P_{max}}$ denotes the pooled contract that maximizes h's financing-*NPV*.

Similar examples can be used to illustrate items (ii) and (iii).

(2) *Nature of the Manager's Private Information.* From Eqs. (12a–12b) and (13a–13c), note that for any contract in $\Omega^C[\theta^x, M, S]$, θ^x determines the difference in payments made by the two firm-types. This, in turn, determines the financing-*NPV*s of these contracts and hence: (i) whether *IA* is costly or costless, (ii) the financing policy when *IA* is costly, and (iii) the range of financing choices when *IA* is costless.

The following example illustrates (i). Suppose that for a particular θ^x, the candidate contracts set contains only contracts with $NPV_h^C(F) < 0$. Again, *IA* is costly (beneficial) to $h(l)$. Now suppose θ^x changes. This changes the financing-*NPV*s of contracts in the candidate contracts set and if now $NPV_h^C(F) = 0$ under one of the contracts, *IA* will be costlessly resolved.

Similar examples can be used to illustrate (ii) and (iii).

(3) *The Security Space.* The security space determines the contracting space and hence the contracts in $\Omega^C[\theta^x, M, S]$. It also determines the difference in payments made by the two firm-types under any contract, and hence their financing-*NPV*s. For these reasons, the security space determines: (i) whether *IA* is costly or costless, (ii) the financing policy when *IA* is costly, and (iii) the range of financing choices when *IA* is costless.

The following example illustrates (i). Suppose that for a particular S, the candidate contracts set for a firm contains only contracts with $NPV_h^C(F) < 0$. Again, *IA* is costly (beneficial) to $h(l)$. Now suppose that S changes. This changes the contracts in the candidate contracts set and their financing-*NPV*s. Now, if $NPV_h^C(F) = 0$ under any one of the contracts, *IA* will be costlessly resolved.

Similar examples can be used to illustrate (ii) and (iii).

Thus, with *IA*, firm policies depend on three primitives: one non firm-specific primitive, S, and two firm-specific primitives, $[M, \theta^x]$. These are the same primitives affecting the manager's and investors' decisions with *IA* (see discussion at end of Chapter 6). In contrast, with symmetric information, none of the primitives — the security space, financing needs, or the firm-type's cash flow distribution — that affect the manager's and investors' decisions impact firm policies.

7.4. Limitations of Analysis

While the preceding discussion has provided some interesting insights, it has some shortcomings.

(1) Our analysis has demonstrated that, depending on the composition of the candidate contracts set, there are two possibilities regarding the cost/benefit of raising capital. The first possibility is that h incurs a cost (while l gains) and the second is that *IA* is costlessly resolved for h (and l).

However, we have not answered the following question(s): Under what parameters $[\theta^x, M]$ and hence under what conditions is *IA* costly/costless? Further, when *IA* is costly, under what conditions is the magnitude of the cost high (low)?

(2) We have also shown that when *IA* is costly and C_h^{Pmax} is viable, financing policy depends on the most concave security. Specifically, we showed that the security issued is (i) the most concave security, if it exists and (ii) depends on the firm's financing needs when the most concave security does not exist.

However, we have not answered the following questions: What are the conditions [i.e., what are the parameters (θ^x, M)] under which the most concave security exists? What are the specific financing choices for a firm if the most concave security does not exist?

(3) We have also shown that financing policy is partially irrelevant for firms for which IA is costlessly resolved.

We have not answered the following question: What is the feasible range of financing choices for such firms?

To draw empirical predictions and implications for managers it is critical that we answer these questions.

Because we have left S unspecified, we cannot as yet do so. It is important to understand why. The key variable determining the answers is the financing-NPV of the contracts in the candidate contracts set. This, in turn, depends jointly on the security space and the firm-specific parameters (θ^x, M). To get interpretable implications, it is therefore necessary to explicitly specify the composition of the security space.

This is precisely what we do in the next chapter. We assume that the security space contains just debt and equity securities. The process that we use to obtain answers for the debt–equity security space can also be used to study any other security space.

Chapter 8

Additional Implications Specific to the Debt–Equity Security Space

8.1. Financing-NPV of Contracts in Candidate Contracts Set

In this chapter we answer the questions posed at the end of the previous chapter under a security space which consists of three securities: (i) zero-coupon (pure) debt, D with $\vec{P}_D = b$, the face value of debt,[1] (ii) (pure) equity, E, with $\vec{P}_E = f$, the fraction of equity value issued to the new investors, and (iii) a combination of senior debt and junior equity, DE, with $\vec{P}_{DE} = b, f$.[2]

---

[1] While our methodology can admit interest-bearing debt, studying this case yields no new insights.

[2] As noted in Part II, we assume limited liability and disallow repurchases. Thus, the only economically meaningful values for b are in the range $[0, \max_{q,\phi} X_q^{\phi}]$ and, for f, are in the range $[0, 1]$.

As discussed, we must begin by identifying the financing-*NPV*s of the contracts in candidate contracts set, $\Omega^C[\theta^x, M, S = \{D, E, DE\}]$. To do so, we exploit the fact that financing-*NPV*s depend on the difference in the value of payments made by the firm-types, $V^s(\tilde{X}_h, \vec{P}_s) - V^s(\tilde{X}_l, \vec{P}_s) \equiv R^s(\theta^x, \vec{P}_s)$. Specifically, the firm-types break even when they make the same payments. However, when the payments made by $h(l)$ exceed those made by $l(h)$, financing-*NPV* for $h(l)$ is negative; the larger the difference between the payments made by the firm-types, the more negative is the financing-*NPV*.

8.1.1. *Financing-NPV of Debt Contracts*

First consider debt contracts. A debt contract's financing-*NPV* depends on the difference in value of payments made by the two firm-types under the debt contract, that is, on $R^D(\theta^x, b)$:

$$R^D(\theta^x, b) \equiv V^D(\tilde{X}_h, b) - V^D(\tilde{X}_l, b). \qquad (14)$$

In Eq. (14), $V^D(\tilde{X}_q, b)$, is the value of the *actual* payments made by firm-type q. This is the value of *promised* payments, b, less the firm's credit risk. Here q's credit risk is a dollar measure and is defined as q's default probability multiplied by the value of the investor's expected loss in default.

The value of *promised* payments is the same for both firm-types. Hence, the *NPV* of debt contracts depends on the difference in the credit risks of the two firm-types, i.e., on *IA* about the firm's credit risk, or simply "credit risk *IA*." Credit risk *IA* is measured as h's credit risk less that of l's and it is equal to the negative of $R^D(\theta^x, b)$. This means that when $R^D(\theta^x, b)$ is positive, credit risk *IA* is negative (and vice versa).

Both the sign of credit risk *IA* and the magnitude of credit risk *IA* ("credit risk spread") matter. Specifically, if both firm-types have the same credit risk, credit risk *IA* is zero and the *NPV* of debt contracts is zero for both firm-types. If h's (l's) credit risk is lower, credit risk *IA* is negative (positive) and the *NPV* of debt contracts is negative for $h(l)$. The lower the credit risk of $h(l)$, the larger is the credit risk spread and the more negative is the *NPV* of h's (l's) debt contracts.

8.1.2. *Financing-NPV of Equity Contracts*

The value of payments made by firm q under an equity contract is fV_q^X. Thus, the *NPV* of equity contracts depends upon the difference in the value of payments made by the two firm-types, $R^E(\theta^x, f)$, where:

$$R^E(\theta^x, f) \equiv V^E(\tilde{X}_h, f) - V^E(\tilde{X}_l, f) = f\left[V_h^X - V_l^X\right]. \quad (15)$$

Here, $\left(V_h^X - V_l^X\right)$ is the *IA* about the firm's value — which we call "value *IA*." The *NPV* of equity contracts thus depends on value *IA*. Value *IA* is positive since h is assumed to be the higher-valued firm. Thus, h will always make larger payments under equity contracts and the *NPV* of equity contracts for h is always negative. The greater the value *IA*, the more negative is the *NPV* of h's equity contracts.

8.1.3. *Financing-NPV of Debt–Equity Contracts*

The value of the payments made by firm q under a debt–equity contract is:

$$V_q^{DE}(b, f) = V_q^D(b) + f\left[V_q^X - V_q^D(b)\right]. \quad (16a)$$

The first term on the right-hand side of this equation is the value of payments from the debt portion of the contract and second is the value accruing from the equity portion. Thus, the financing-*NPV* of debt–equity contracts depends upon $R^{DE}(\theta^x, b, f)$ where:

$$R^{DE}(\theta^x, b, f) \equiv V_h^{DE}(b, f) - V_l^{DE}(b, f)$$
$$= R^D(\theta^x, b)(1 - f) + R^E(\theta^x, f). \quad (16b)$$

Equation (16b) shows that the *NPV* of debt–equity contracts depends on both credit risk *IA* and value *IA*. When credit risk *IA* is positive [$R^D(\theta^x, b)$ is negative] and its spread is large enough to exactly offset the positive $R^E(\theta^x, f)$, the *NPV* of the contract is zero for both firm-types. When credit risk *IA* is positive and its spread is large enough to more than offset the positive $R^E(\theta^x, f)$, the financing-*NPV* for *l* is negative. In all other situations, the *NPV* for *h* is negative. The preceding discussion is summarized in Proposition 7.

Proposition 7 (*Financing-NPVs of Contracts*). Credit risk *IA* and value *IA* are the two primitives that determine the financing-*NPV*s of contracts under the debt-equity security space. Credit risk *IA* determines the financing-*NPV* for debt and value *IA* determines the financing-*NPV* for equity.

The extant literature, following Myers-Majluf, has long recognized that value *IA* is a key determinant of financing-*NPV* of equity contracts. Further, it has viewed *IA* about the variance of the firm's cash flows or "variance *IA*" (the difference in the variances of *h*'s and *l*'s cash flows) to be the determinant of the financing-*NPV* of debt contracts.

Although similar, there are several important differences between variance *IA* and credit risk *IA*. For example, a firm can have zero variance *IA*, and a non-zero credit risk *IA*. This means that *NPV* of debt financing can be positive/negative even when there is no variance *IA*. Also, whereas the magnitude of variance *IA* is affected similarly by "downside *IA*" (*IA* regarding the downside cash flows) and "upside *IA*" (*IA* regarding the upside cash flows), the magnitude of credit risk *IA* (credit risk spread) is more sensitive to downside *IA*. This means that the *NPV* of debt financing depends more on downside *IA* than on upside *IA*. Third, the ordering of credit risk and variance of the firm-types need not be the same. A firm-type, say *h*, may have higher variance than l because of larger cash flows in the upside. Its credit risk may, however, be lower because it also has larger cash flows in the downside.

We next answer the three sets of questions posed at the end of Chapter 7. As will be seen, this analysis yields new results and helps explain some of the conflicting results in existing literature. This is because we have shifted the focus away from variance IA and on to credit risk IA.

8.2. Cost of IA (Question Set 1)

In the previous chapter, we showed that with IA, h incurs a cost (while l gains) when $NPV_h^C(F) < 0$ under all contracts in the candidate contracts set; otherwise IA is costlessly resolved. Further, when IA is costly, the magnitude of the cost depends on the magnitude of $NPV_h^C(F)$ under the $C_h^{P_{max}}$ contract.

Here, we go further and answer the following two interrelated questions under the debt–equity security space: Under what conditions [i.e., parameters (θ^x, M)] is IA costly? When is the magnitude of this cost high?

To answer the first question, we must determine the conditions under which $NPV_h^C(F) < 0$ under all contracts. To answer the second, we must examine the magnitude of $NPV_h^C(F)$ under the $C_h^{P_{max}}$ contract. In this regard, we rely on the preceding discussion regarding the financing-NPVs of debt and equity contracts. The next proposition provides the results of this analysis.

Proposition 8 (*Costless and Costly IA*). If θ^x of a firm is such that:

(i) Credit risk IA is negative for all $b \leq Max(X_l^\phi)$, IA is costly for h regardless of M. Firm h's cost of raising capital increases with increases in credit risk spread, value IA, and the firm's financing need.

(ii) Credit risk *IA* is non-negative for all $b \leq Max(X_l^\phi)$, *IA* is costless regardless of the firm's financing needs, *M*.

(iii) Credit risk *IA* does not satisfy (i) and (ii), *M* determines whether *IA* is costless or costly. When *M* is small (large), *IA* is costless (costly). Further, the likelihood that *IA* is costless (costly) is non-decreasing (non-increasing) in credit risk *IA* and non-increasing (non-decreasing) in value *IA*.

Proof. See Appendix.

Proposition 8 yields four important insights. First, the sign of credit risk *IA* is the key determinant of whether *IA* is costly or costless. To see why, note that it is the sign of financing-*NPV*s of pooled and no-loss contracts that determine whether *IA* is costless or not. From Eqs. (14)–(16) it is apparent that the sign of financing-*NPV* depends upon the sign of credit risk *IA* and value *IA*. Since *h* is assumed to be the higher-valued firm, the sign of value *IA* is always positive. However, credit risk *IA* can be positive, negative, or zero. Thus, it is the sign of credit risk *IA* that plays the key role in determining the sign of financing-*NPV*s and hence of whether *IA* is costless or costly.

Second, *IA* is costly (costless) for a firm if its credit risk *IA* is negative (positive or zero). The intuition is as follows. The $NPV_h^C(F) < 0$ for all equity contracts since value *IA* is always positive. Further, $NPV_h^C(F) < 0$ for all debt and debt–equity contracts if credit risk *IA* is negative, but $NPV_h^C(F) = 0$ for debt and debt–equity contracts if credit risk *IA* is positive or zero [see discussion following Eqs. (14) and (16b)]. This means that if credit risk *IA* is negative, $NPV_h^C(F) < 0$ for all contracts and thus *IA* is costly; however, if credit risk *IA* is positive or zero, there exists a contract with $NPV_h^C(F) = 0$ and *IA* is costlessly resolved.

Third, of the two firm-specific variables, θ^x and *M*, the key parameter that determines whether *IA* is costless or costly is the firm's θ^x. This is because θ^x determines the sign of the credit

risk IA [recall that credit risk IA is the negative of $R^D(\theta^x, b)$].
This insight also explains why Heinkel (1982) finds that IA can
be costlessly resolved while Myers–Majluf find that IA is costly.
Heinkel assumes a θ^x under which the higher-valued firm has a
greater credit risk i.e., credit risk IA is positive. On the other
hand, Myers–Majluf assume a θ^x under which the higher valued
firm has lower credit risk i.e., credit risk IA is negative.

Finally, the preceding discussion does not mean that the
firm's financing need, M, is irrelevant. It matters when credit
risk IA is negative and when the sign of credit risk IA changes.
In the former situation, M determines the magnitude of the cost
of IA. In the latter situation, M determines whether IA is costly
or costless.

8.3. Financing Policy when *IA* is Costly (Question Set 2)

From Proposition 8, IA is costly for h when C_h^{Pmax} is viable
and: (i) if credit risk IA is negative for all $b \leq Max(X_l^\phi)$, or
(ii) if credit risk IA is negative for some $b \leq Max(X_l^\phi)$ and non-
negative for some other face values, and financing needs are high.
From the previous chapter, we know that such firms choose the
C_h^{Pmax} contract and their financing policy is determined by the
security associated with this contract. This security is the most
concave security. If the most concave security does not exist, the
security associated with the C_h^{Pmax} contract depends on M.

Next, we answer the following interrelated questions:

(i) What are the conditions under which the most concave secu-
    rity exists? When is this security debt? When is it equity?
(ii) What are the firm's financing choices when the most concave
    security does not exist? When is the firm's financing choice
    debt? When is it equity?

We address each question separately.

8.3.1. *Existence of the Most Concave Security*

By definition, the most concave security is the security that has the smallest second derivative, $\frac{\partial^2 NPV_h^C(F)}{\partial A^2}$ across all pooled contracts in S. Thus, to identify whether the most concave security exists (and to determine its identity) we must first determine $\frac{\partial^2 NPV_h^C(F)}{\partial A^2}$ for all pooled contracts associated with each security in S.

First, consider debt pooled contracts. The value of the investor's payments under a debt contract made by firm-type q is $V_q^D(b)$. From Eq. (12a) it follows that the NPV for debt contracts, $NPV_h^C(F) = -\pi_l[R^D(\theta^x, b)] = -\pi_l\left[V_h^D(b) - V_l^D(b)\right]$. From Eq. (8) the capital provided under a debt pooled contracts, $A = \sum_q \pi_q V_q^D(b)$. Differentiating $NPV_h^C(F)$ and A with respect to b and using the chain rule yields the derivative of $NPV_h^C(F)$ w.r.t. A. It is seen to be:

$$\frac{\partial NPV_h^C(F)}{\partial A} = -\pi_l \frac{\partial b}{\partial A} * \frac{\partial R^D(\theta^x, b)}{\partial b}$$

$$= \frac{\pi_l}{(1 + r_f)} \frac{\partial b}{\partial A} [F_h(\tilde{X}_h, b) - F_l(\tilde{X}_l, b)], \quad (17a)$$

where

$$\frac{\partial b}{\partial A} = \frac{1 + r_f}{1 - \pi_h F_h(\tilde{X}_h, b) - \pi_l F_l(\tilde{X}_l, b)} > 0.$$

In Eq. (17a), $F_q(\tilde{X}_q, b)$, or simply $F_q(b)$, is firm q's default probability at a promised debt payment. By definition, default probability is less than or equal to 1. Differentiating (17a) with respect to A shows that the second derivative of $NPV_h^C(F)$ w.r.t. A is:

$$\frac{\partial^2 NPV_h^C(F)}{\partial A^2} = a\left[\varphi_h(\tilde{X}_h, b) - \varphi_l(\tilde{X}_l, b)\right]$$

$$\times (1 - F_h(\tilde{X}_h, b))(1 - F_l(\tilde{X}_l, b)), \quad (17b)$$

where

$$a = \frac{\partial b}{\partial A} \frac{\pi_l}{\left[1 - \pi_h F_h(\tilde{X}_h, b) - \pi_l F_l(\tilde{X}_l, b)\right]^2} > 0,$$

and $\varphi_q(\tilde{X}_q, b) = \frac{F_q'(\tilde{X}_q, b)}{1 - F_q(\tilde{X}_q, b)}$ is firm q's hazard rate or conditional (on the probability of survival) default density function evaluated at debt face value b.

Define "hazard rate *IA*," $R^\varphi(\theta^x, b)$, as the hazard rate for firm h less the hazard rate for l. That is, $R^\varphi(\theta^x, b) \equiv \varphi_h(\tilde{X}_h, b) - \varphi_l(\tilde{X}_l, b)$. Equation (17b) shows that a graph of $NPV_h^C(F)$ and A for debt pooled contracts depends on the sign of $R^\varphi(\theta^x, b)$ for $b > 0$.[3] If hazard rate *IA* is positive (negative), $\frac{\partial^2 NPV_h^C(F)}{\partial A^2}$ is positive (negative) and the graph is convex (concave). If hazard rate *IA* is zero, it is linear. Finally, if the sign of $R^\varphi(\theta^x, b)$ changes across b, the graph can be concavo-convex, convexo-concave, etc.

Next consider equity contracts. For these contracts, the value of payments made by a firm-type is fV_q^X and an analysis similar to that of debt reveals that:

$$\frac{\partial NPV_h^C(F)}{\partial A} = -\pi_l \frac{V_h^X - V_l^X}{A^{Pmax}}. \tag{18}$$

Thus a graph for $NPV_h^C(F)$ is linear and decreasing in A for equity pooled contracts.

Finally, consider pooled debt–equity contracts. The financing terms of debt–equity contracts have two parameters, b and f. We first analyze the graph for all contracts with the same face value, say b_1. An analysis similar to that of debt contracts

---

[3]In Eqs. (17a) and (17b), the derivative of $NPV_h^C(F)$ exists only for $b > 0$. For this reason, we only analyze the sign of hazard rate *IA* for $b > 0$. Further, if $F_q(b) = 1$ for any b, hazard rate *IA* is undefined. For such bs, we examine the sign of $[F_h'(b)(1 - F_l(b)) - F_l'(b)(1 - F_h(b))]$.

shows that:

- The graph for $NPV_h^C(F)$ is linear in A.
- The starting point of the graph is when the debt–equity contract has $f = 0$. At this point, $A = \sum_q \pi_q V_q^D(b_1)$ and $NPV_h^C(F) = -\pi_l \left[V_h^D(b_1) - V_l^D(b_1) \right]$.
- The ending point of the graph is when the debt–equity contract has $f = 1$. At this point, $A = A^{Pmax}$ and $NPV_h^C(F) = -\pi_l \left(V_h^X - V_l^X \right)$. Note that the end point is independent of b_1.

The graph of $NPV_h^C(F)$ versus A for pooled debt–equity contracts with any other face value is similarly linear.

Since the graph of equity and debt–equity contracts is linear, the preceding discussion implies that it is the shape of the graph for debt contracts, and thus the sign of the hazard rate IA, that is the key determinant of the most concave security.

If hazard rate IA is negative (positive), the most concave security exists and it is debt (equity). The firm thus chooses a debt (equity) contract. If hazard rate IA is zero, both debt and equity are equally concave (both are linear) and the firm is indifferent between the two. Finally, if the sign of hazard rate IA changes across b, the most concave security does not exist. In this situation, the security accepted depends on M. Summarizing,

Proposition 9 (*IA is Costly: Most Concave Security*). If θ^x is such that the sign of hazard rate IA, $R^\varphi(\theta^x, b)$:

(a) Does not change across b, the most concave security exists.

    (i) If $R^\varphi(\theta^x, b) \leq 0$ for all $b > 0$ (with strict inequality for at least one b), debt is the most concave security. The firm chooses a debt contract for all M.

    (ii) If $R^\varphi(\theta^x, b) = 0$ for all $b > 0$, debt and equity are equally concave. The firm is indifferent between a debt and equity contract for all M.

    (iii) If $R^\varphi(\theta^x, b) \geq 0$ for all $b > 0$ (with strict inequality for at least one b), equity is the most concave security. The firm chooses an equity contract for all M.

(b) Changes with b, the most concave security does not exist. The firm, depending on M, picks a debt contract, an equity contract, or a debt–equity contract.

Proposition 9 yields three key insights. First, it shows that the hazard rate IA is the key determinant of the manager's financing choice when IA is costly.[4] It should be noted that hazard rate IA is very closely related to credit risk IA; specifically, it depends on the second derivative of credit risk IA w.r.t. A.

Second, of the two firm-specific variables θ^x and M, θ^x is the key parameter that determines the financing choice when IA is costly. This is because θ^x determines the sign of the hazard rate IA, $R^\varphi(\theta^x, b)$. This insight explains why Innes (1993) finds debt to be optimal but Noe (1988) does not. Innes assumes a θ^x under which the higher-valued firm has a lower hazard rate, i.e., hazard rate IA is negative.[5] On the other hand, Noe (1988) considers a θ^x under which the higher-valued firm can have a higher hazard rate.[6]

---

[4]Nachman and Noe (1994), have also recognized the importance of hazard rate IA for the firm's debt–equity decision.

[5]Innes (1993) assumes higher-type firms have 'better' cash flow distributions in the sense of the monotone likelihood ratio property (MLRP). See Milgrom (1981) for distributional specifications satisfying MLRP.

[6]Noe (1988) not only considers a different θ^x but also allows for more firm-types than Myers and Majluf (1984). He does not address whether his results obtain because he considers a different θ^x or a different number of firm-types. Our analysis implies that his results arise because he has assumed a different θ^x, not because he has multiple firm-types.

Finally, this discussion does not mean that the firm's financing need, M, is irrelevant. As seen, M affects the firm's financing choices, but only when the sign of hazard rate IA changes.

8.3.2. *Financing Choices When the Most Concave Security does Not Exist*

When the sign of hazard rate IA changes, the most concave security does not exist and the firm's financing policy is ambiguous.

In this situation, when will a firm choose a debt contract? An equity contract? We answer this by examining how the two firm-specific primitives, $[M, \theta^x]$ affect the security associated with the C_h^{Pmax} contract (the contract chosen by the firm). We obtain two results.

The first result relates to how M affects the security associated with the C_h^{Pmax} contract. It shows that the impact of M on the security associated with the C_h^{Pmax} contract depends on θ^x. Specifically,

Proposition 10a (*IA is Costly: Financing Needs and Security Issued*).   Suppose θ^x is such that:

(i) $R^\varphi(\theta^x, b) > 0$ at low b and $R^\varphi(\theta^x, b) < 0$ at high b. The security associated with the C_h^{Pmax} contract is debt (equity) if M is large (small).

(ii) $R^\varphi(\theta^x, b) < 0$ at low b and $R^\varphi(\theta^x, b) > 0$ at high b. The security associated with the C_h^{Pmax} contract is debt–equity (debt) if M is high (low).

Proof. See Appendix.

It is useful to contrast this result with that in Garcia *et al.* (2013). These authors find that firms are more likely to choose an equity (debt) contract when financing needs are large (small). However, our analysis clearly demonstrates that their result cannot be generalized across all firms. For some firms, it is equally plausible that the firm issues debt (equity) if financing needs are large (small).

The second result relates to how θ^x affects the security associated with the $C_h^{P_{max}}$ contract. Specifically, it identifies the θ^x under which the likelihood of an equity contract (with or without debt) being chosen is larger. Assume that value of both h and l remains fixed.

Proposition 10b (*IA is Costly: Equity Issuance and Credit Risk Spread*). If θ^x is such that the sign of hazard rate *IA* changes with b and the credit risk spread is large, the security associated with the $C_h^{P_{max}}$ contract is more likely to be equity or debt–equity. The firm is more likely to choose an equity or debt–equity contract.

The proof/intuition is as follows. Suppose that at a particular M, h's financing-NPV is highest under debt (as compared to the financing-NPV under equity and debt–equity contracts). The firm will choose a debt contract. Now suppose that the credit risk spread increases while the values of both h and l (and thus value *IA*) remains fixed. Then, h's financing-NPV under debt decreases while its financing-NPV under equity is unaffected. The financing-NPV under debt–equity also decreases, but only for the part raised through debt financing. If the credit risk spread increases sufficiently, h's financing-NPV under debt can be lower than the financing-NPV under equity and debt–equity contracts and the firm will issue equity (with or without debt). This, in turn, increases the likelihood of equity issuance.

Proposition 10b raises a question. What are the characteristics of firms for which the credit risk spread is larger? To answer this question we consider a binomial world with two t_1 states, up-state, u, and down-state, d, with probabilities π^u and π^d respectively. We assume that the cash flows for h and l in the up-state are either the same or exceed those in the down-state. Note here that downside (upside) IA is h's cash flows in the down-state (up-state) less those of l's. We find that:

Proposition 10c (*Characteristics of Firms Choosing Contracts with Equity*). Firms with high risk and those for which a greater proportion of value IA comes from downside IA are more likely to choose a contract that contains equity (either with or without debt).

Proof. See Appendix.

In this proposition, risk refers to the volatility common to both firm-types, not the volatility that affects just one firm-type. Thus a change in risk affects the cash flows of both types identically.

The intuition for the proposition is as follows. First, consider the impact of risk. As risk increases, the credit risk for both firm-types also increases. However, l's credit risk increases more since l is more likely to default (here l has a higher or the same credit risk as h). This increases the credit risk spread and thus the likelihood of a contract with equity being chosen.

Next consider downside IA. Note that the value of a firm's cash flows comes from the upside and the downside. There are thus two sources of value IA — downside IA and upside IA. A firm-type's credit risk is more sensitive to downside IA than it is to upside IA. Consequently, firms for which a large proportion of value IA comes from the downside IA will have a larger credit risk spread and they are thus more likely to choose a contract that contains equity.

8.4. Financing Policy When *IA* is Costless (Question 3)

From Proposition 8, *IA* is costless for a firm if its: (i) credit risk *IA* is non-negative for all $b \leq Max(X_l^\phi)$, or (ii) credit risk *IA* is non-negative for some $b \leq Max(X_l^\phi)$ and negative for some other face values, and financing needs are low. From the previous chapter, we know that each firm-type can pick any contract in $\Omega^C[\theta^x, M, S]$ for which $NPV_q^C(F) = 0$ and the financing-NPV is non-positive for the other firm-type. Consequently, financing policy is partially irrelevant in the sense that it is flexible, but only within a feasible range.

We next answer the following question under the debt–equity security space: What is the feasible range of financing choices for such firms? For both (i) and (ii), the answer to this question is qualitatively similar. Therefore, we only focus on the first case, i.e., the case where credit risk *IA* is non-negative for all face values.

Using Eqs. (14)–(16) we answer this question for each type q by determining the $(s, \vec{P}_s)$ of all the contracts for which (i) $NPV_q^C(F) = 0$ and (ii) the financing-NPV is non-positive for the other firm-type. The results are summarized in the next proposition.

Proposition 11a (*Financing Policies When IA is Cost-less*). Firm h issues: (i) debt contracts with $R^D(\theta^x, b) = 0$ or $R^D(\theta^x, b) < 0$ or (ii) debt–equity contracts with $f \leq \bar{f} = R^D(\theta^x, b)/[R^D(\theta^x, b) - (V_h^X - V_l^X)]$. Firm l issues: (i) debt contracts with $R^D(\theta^x, b) = 0$, (ii) equity contracts, or (iii) debt–equity contracts with $f \geq \bar{f} = R^D(\theta^x, b)/[R^D(\theta^x, b) - (V_h^X - V_l^X)]$.

Proof. See Appendix.

Proposition 11a yields five insights. First, of the two firm-specific variables θ^x and M, θ^x is the key parameter that determines the financing choice when IA is costless. This is because θ^x determines $R^D(\theta^x, b)$ and the difference in values of the cash flows, $V_h^X - V_l^X$.[7]

Second, the feasible range of financing choices for each firm-type is as follows. Firm-type h can choose any debt contract or any debt–equity contract with $f \leq \bar{f}$ but it will not choose equity or debt–equity contracts with $f > \bar{f}$. Firm-type l can choose any equity contract, any debt contract with $R^D(\theta^x, b) = 0$, or any debt–equity contract with $f \geq \bar{f}$ but it will not choose a debt contract with $R^D(\theta^x, b) < 0$ or debt–equity contracts with $f < \bar{f}$.

Third, similar to Heinkel (1982), h picks a debt–equity contract with less equity than the one picked by l. The intuition is as follows. When credit risk IA is non-negative, h's payments for debt are lower than l's. Further, since h has a higher value, l's payments for equity are lower. This means that h's NPV under a debt–equity contract is higher when there is more debt and less equity. On the other hand, l's NPV is higher when there is less debt and more equity. Since each firm-type picks the contract under which its NPV is higher, it follows that h

---

[7]This does not mean that M has no impact on financing choice when IA is costless. To see this, recall that IA is costless in two situations: (i) credit risk IA is non-negative for all $b \leq Max(X_l^\phi)$, or (ii) credit risk IA is non-negative for some $b \leq Max(X_l^\phi)$ and negative for some other face values and financing needs are low. In the first situation — which is being discussed here — M does not matter. In the second situation, however, M does matter. We do not demonstrate and explore the implications of this finding because our model yields no insight as to *how* M affects financing policy.

chooses a debt–equity contract with less equity than the one picked by l.

Fourth, if the firm chooses a debt–equity contract, the amount of equity in this contract is an increasing function of $\bar{f}$. To see why, note from the Proposition that $f \leq \bar{f}$ if h chooses a debt–equity contract, and $f \geq \bar{f}$ if l chooses the contract. This implies that as $\bar{f}$ increases, (i) h *can* pick contracts with more equity and (ii) l will pick contracts with more equity.

Fifth, since $\bar{f}$ depends on credit risk IA and value IA ($V_h^X - V_l^X$), so will the amount of equity contained in the debt–equity contract. The next proposition shows how.

Proposition 11b (*Amount of Equity and the Primitives*). The greater the credit risk spread and/or the lower the value IA due to lower (higher) cash flow for $h(l)$, the greater is the amount of equity contained in the firm's chosen debt–equity contract.

Proof. See Appendix.

Proposition 11b raises a question. What are the characteristics of firms for which credit risk spread is larger and/or value IA is lower? The proof of the next proposition shows these are firms with large magnitude of downside IA and large risk. As with Proposition 10c, we demonstrate this result in a binomial world.

Proposition 11c (*Characteristics of Firms Choosing Large Amounts of Equity*). Firms with high risk and a large magnitude of downside IA choose debt–equity contracts with larger amounts of equity.

Proof. See Appendix.

The underlying intuition is as follows.[8] First consider the effect of the magnitude of downside *IA* on equity issuance. Since we are considering firms where credit risk *IA* is non-negative, it follows that l's cash flows in the downside are greater than or equal to h's (i.e., downside *IA* is negative). Thus, the magnitude of downside *IA* is large if l's (h's) cash flows in the downside are large (small). In this case, credit risk spread is large and value *IA* is small. Thus, these firms will choose debt–equity contracts with larger amounts of equity.

Next consider the effect of risk. Suppose that the volatility of the cash flows of both firm-types increases by the same amount either because economic risk or the risk of the firm's assets increases. In this situation, the credit risk for both firm-types increases. However, it increases h's credit risk more since h is more likely to default (recall that here h has a higher or the same credit risk as l). This increases the credit risk spread. Thus, firms with larger risk will choose debt–equity contracts with larger amounts of equity.

Summarizing, when *IA* is costless, firms with high risk and large magnitude of downside *IA* will choose debt–equity contracts with large amounts of equity.

Table 2 summarizes this chapter's findings.

In the next chapter, we illustrate, using numerical examples, this chapter's key financing policy results.

Note that there two sets of financing policy results: one for positive credit risk *IA* and the other for negative credit risk *IA*. It is more likely that credit risk and value are inversely related (credit risk *IA* is negative). In the interest of space, we

---

[8]Propositions 11c and 10c are similar in that both pertain to equity issued. However, Proposition 11c is about the amount of equity issued as part of the debt–equity contracts, while Proposition 10c is about the likelihood that equity (with or without debt) is issued.

Table 2. *IA* implications when *S* contains just debt and equity.

I. If the firm parameter, θ^x is such that:	II. Investment policy	III. Financing policy	IV. Financing cost/benefit
Credit risk *IA* is negative for all $b \leq Max(X_l^\phi)$ and $C_h^{P_{max}}$ is:	Economically viable for *h*	Depending on the sign of hazard rate *IA*, the most concave security is debt or equity. Equity issuance (with or without debt) can be optimal	*h* loses while *l* gains
		Firms with high risk and those for which a larger proportion of value *IA* comes from the downside *IA* are more likely to choose a contract containing equity[a]	*h*'s cost and *l*'s gain increase as: (i) credit risk spread increases, and (ii) the value *IA* increases

(*Continued*)

Note: In this table: (i) credit risk *IA* is the difference between the credit risks of *h* and *l*, (ii) credit risk spread is the magnitude of credit risk *IA*, (iii) value *IA* is the difference in the firm value of *h* and *l*, (iv) $C_h^{P_{max}}$ is the pooled contract that maximizes *h*'s financing-*NPV*, and (v) hazard rate *IA* is the difference in hazard rates for the two firm-types.

[a]These financing policy results also hold for firms if credit risk *IA* is negative for some $b \leq Max(X_l^\phi)$ and non-negative for some other face values and financing needs are high.

Table 2. (*Continued*)

I. If the firm parameter, θ^x is such that:	II. Investment policy	III. Financing policy	IV. Financing cost/benefit
Not economically viable for h	Only l invests; h does not.	h: Retains existing capital structure l: Completely irrelevant in the Modigliani–Miller (1958) sense	h: Does not raise external capital l: Breaks even
Credit risk IA is positive or zero for all $b \le Max(X_l^\phi)$	Both firm-types invest in the project.	Partially irrelevant: h enters into any debt or any debt–equity contract with $f = (0, \bar{f}]$ and l issues only debt contracts with $R^D(\theta^x, b) = 0$, any equity contract, or any debt–equity contract with $f = [\bar{f}, 1)^{\text{b}}$ Firms with high risk and large magnitude of downside IA will choose a debt–equity contract with large amounts of equity	Both firm-types break even

[b]As noted earlier, $\bar{f} = R^D(\theta^x, b)/[R^D(\theta^x, b) - (V_h^X - V_l^X)]$.

therefore only illustrate the financing policy results for firms with negative credit risk *IA*. The results for the negative credit risk *IA* case are summarized in Propositions 9, 10a, and 10c. For the convenience of the reader, we restate these propositions before illustrating them with numerical examples.

Chapter 9

Numerical Illustrations of Key Financing Policy Results under the Debt–Equity Security Space

9.1. Illustrating Results for Proposition 9

For firms with negative credit risk IA, IA is costly and the firm chooses the $C_h^{P_{max}}$ contract, i.e., the contract that maximizes h's financing-NPV. The security associated with this contract is the most concave security. However, the most concave security may not exist. In this situation, the security associated with the $C_h^{P_{max}}$ contract depends on the firm's financing needs.

Proposition 9 describes the conditions under which the concave security exists and reveals its identity. Specifically, it shows that if the hazard rate IA, $R^{\varphi}(\theta^x, b)$:

(i) Is negative for all b, debt is the most concave security and hence is the security associated with $C_h^{P_{max}}$. The firm chooses a debt contract.

(ii) Is zero for all b, debt and equity are equally concave. There are multiple C_h^{Pmax} contracts — one with debt, one with equity, and many debt–equity contracts. The firm is indifferent between debt and equity.

(iii) Is positive for all b, equity is the most concave security and hence is the security associated with C_h^{Pmax}. The firm chooses an equity contract.

(iv) Changes sign with b, the most concave security does not exist. Depending on M, the security associated with C_h^{Pmax} can be debt, equity, or debt–equity.

We next illustrate each of these results with numerical examples. In each we assume that $r_f = 0$ and that each firm-type is equally likely ($\pi_h = \pi_l = 0.5$).

9.1.1. *Hazard Rate IA is Negative (The Most Concave Security Exists and It is Debt)*

At t_0, the firm has \$20 in slack and an investment opportunity that requires a \$60 investment. Thus, the firm must raise \$40 in capital if it wants to invest in the project.

There are two equi-probable states (up-state, u, and down-state, d) at t_1 and the total cum-project cash flows of h and l in these states are:

Cum-project cash flows, X_q^ϕ

	Down-state $(\phi = d)$	Up-state $(\phi = u)$
Higher-valued firm $(q = h)$	\$210	\$250
Lower-valued firm $(q = l)$	\$0	\$140

The value of h's cash flows, $V_h^X = \$230$ and the value of l's cash flows, $V_l^X = \$70$.

In this example, note that the minimum cash flows of h exceed the maximum cash flows of l. Under this θ^x, it is easily verified that hazard rate IA is negative. According to Proposition 9, debt is the most concave security, and hence is the security associated with the contract that maximizes h's financing-NPV, $NPV_h^C(F)$.

To see if this is indeed the case, we need to plot a graph of $NPV_h^C(F)$ versus A for pooled debt, pooled equity, and the pooled debt–equity contracts.

9.1.1.1. Graph of $NPV_h^C(F)$ versus A for pooled contracts

Plotting the graph requires calculating the $NPV_h^C(F)$ and A under pooled contracts for each security s and each financing term $\vec{P}_s$. The value of $NPV_h^C(F)$ and A under one $(s, \vec{P}_s)$ yields one point on the graph.

We next demonstrate the process for determining one such point at $s = D$ (debt) and financing term, $b(face\ value) = \$30$.

Step 1: *Determine the t_1 cash flows to the investor, $X_q^\phi(s, \vec{P}_s)$, from each firm-type in each state.* Under a debt contract, $X_q^\phi(s, \vec{P}_s) = min(X_q^\phi, b)$. At $b = \$30$, the cash flows to the investor from each firm-type in each state are:

Cash flows to the investor, $X_q^\phi(s, \vec{P}_s)$

	Down-state ($\phi = d$)	Up-state ($\phi = u$)
Higher-valued firm ($q = h$)	$30	$30
Lower-valued firm ($q = l$)	$0	$30

Step 2: *Determine the t_0 value of the cash flows to the investor, $V_q^s(\vec{P}_s)$, from each firm-type.* Since $r_f = 0$ and the two states are equally likely, value of h's cash flows, $V_h^s(\vec{P}_s) = \$30$ and that of l's, $V_l^s(\vec{P}_s) = \$15$.

Step 3: *Determine $A = \sum_q \pi_q V^s(\tilde{X}_q, \vec{P}_s)$ and $NPV_h^C(F) = -\pi_l[V^s(\tilde{X}_h, \vec{P}_s) - V^s(\tilde{X}_l, \vec{P}_s)]$.* Under the debt contract,

$$A = 0.5 * 30 + 0.5 * 15 = \$22.5 \text{ and } NPV_h^C(F) = -0.5$$
$$[30 - 15] = -\$7.5.$$

Thus, one point on the graph of $NPV_h^C(F)$ versus A is ($22.5, -$7.5). One can determine the remaining points on the graph by similarly calculating the $NPV_h^C(F)$ and A for every other $(s, \vec{P}_s)$. This yields the following graph (for debt–equity contracts we only plot the contracts at face value $b = \$50$). Note, as Proposition 6b shows, that the end point of the graph for each security is $A = A^{P_{max}} = \sum_q \pi_q V_q^X = \$150$ and $NPV_h^C(F) = -\pi_l(V_h^X - V_l^X) = -\$80$.

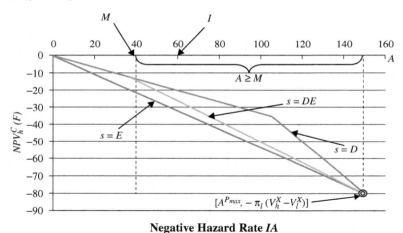

Negative Hazard Rate *IA*

9.1.1.2. Verification of result

The graph above clearly demonstrates that debt is the most concave security. As such, it is the security associated with $C_h^{P_{max}}$. The firm therefore chooses a debt contract.

9.1.2. *Hazard Rate IA is Zero (Indifference between Debt and Equity)*

At t_0, the firm must again raise $40 to take on the project. There are three equi-probable states (up-state, u, middle-state, m, and down-state, d) next period. The total cum-project cash flows of h and l in these states are:

Cum-project cash flows, X_q^ϕ

	Down-state ($\phi = d$)	Middle-state ($\phi = m$)	Up-state ($\phi = u$)
h	$0	$300	$300
l	$0	$0	$300

The value of h's cash flows, $V_h^X = \$200$ and the value of l's cash flows, $V_l^X = \$100$.

In this example, there are two possible cash flow outcomes and there is IA only about the probability of each outcome (not about cash flow magnitudes). Under this θ^x, it is easily verified that hazard rate IA is zero. According to Proposition 9, debt and equity are equally concave (both are linear). This can be readily seen from the following graph (for debt–equity contracts, we only plot the contracts at face value $b = \$50$).

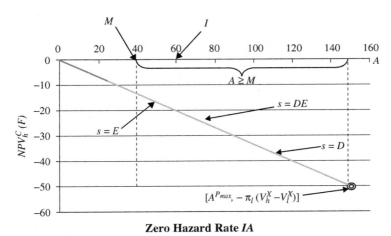

Zero Hazard Rate *IA*

The firm is therefore indifferent between debt and equity.[1]

---

[1]In this situation, it is well known [see e.g., Tirole (2006)] that debt and equity are equivalent.

9.1.3. *Hazard Rate IA is Positive (Most Concave Security Exists and It is Equity)*

Once again, at t_0, the firm must raise \$40 in capital to take on the project. There are two equi-probable states (u and d) next period. In this example, the cum-project cash flows for h and l are:

Cum-project cash flows, X_q^ϕ

	Down-state ($\phi = d$)	Up-state ($\phi = u$)
h	\$100	\$250
l	\$0	\$250

The value of h's cash flows, $V_h^X = \$175$ and the value of l's cash flows, $V_l^X = \$125$.

In this example, there is a downside $IA \equiv X_h^d - X_l^d = \$100 - \$0 = \$100$. However, upside $IA \equiv X_h^u - X_l^u = \$250 - \$250 = \$0$. Under this θ^x, it is easily verified that hazard rate IA is positive. According to Proposition 9, equity is the most concave security in this situation. This can be readily seen from the following graph (for debt–equity contracts, we only plot the contracts at face value $b = \$50$).

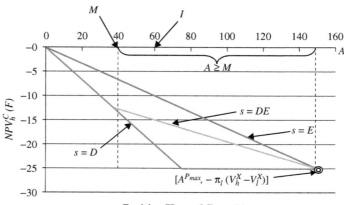

Positive Hazard Rate *IA*

The firm therefore chooses an equity contract.

9.1.4. *Hazard Rate IA Sign Changes (Most Concave Security does Not Exist and Security Issued Depends on Financing Needs)*

At t_0, the firm has an investment opportunity requiring $100. There are two equi-probable states (u and d) next period. In this case, the cum-project cash flows for h and l are:

Cum-project cash flows, X_q^ϕ

	Down-state ($\phi = d$)	Up-state ($\phi = u$)
h	$50	$300
l	$0	$250

The value of h's cash flows, $V_h^X = \$175$ and the value of l's cash flows, $V_l^X = \$125$.

In this example, there is both downside $IA \equiv X_h^d - X_l^d = \$50 - \$0 = \$50$, and upside $IA \equiv X_h^u - X_l^u = \$300 - \$250 = \$50$. Under this θ^x, it is easily verified that hazard rate IA is first positive and then negative.

According to Proposition 9, the most concave security does not exist in this situation. This can be readily seen from the following graph (for debt–equity contracts, we only plot the contracts at face value $b = \$50$).

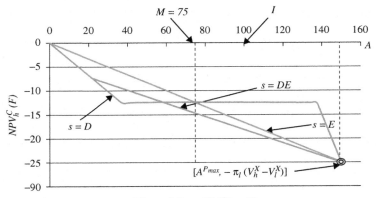

Hazard Rate *IA* Sign Changes

Thus, the security associated with C_h^{Pmax} depends on the firm's financing needs, M. When $M > \$75$, debt is the security with C_h^{Pmax} and when $M < \$75$ equity is the security. When $M = \$75$, both debt and equity maximize h's financing-NPV and hence the firm is indifferent between the two.

For these firms, the debt–equity choice cannot be unambiguously determined. Two results are useful in this regard. The first result is Proposition 10a and the second is Proposition 10c. We next illustrate these results with examples. We continue to assume that $r_f = 0$ and that each firm-type is equally likely ($\pi_h = \pi_l = 0.5$).

9.2. Illustrating Results for Proposition 10a

This proposition shows that the impact of M on the firm's debt–equity choice depends on θ^x.

9.2.1. *Hazard Rate IA is First Positive then Negative (Firm Issues Debt if M is High and Equity if It is Low)*

The previous example illustrates this result. As noted, in that example, hazard rate *IA* is first positive and then negative. Further, consistent with Proposition 10a, debt is issued when M is high (greater than \$75) and equity is issued when M is low (less than \$75).

9.2.2. *Hazard Rate IA is First Negative then Positive (Firm Issues Debt if M is Low and Debt-Equity if It is High)*

Again, at t_0, the firm has an investment opportunity requiring \$100. There are three equi-probable states (up-state, u, middle-state, m, down-state, d) next period and the total cum-project cash flows of h and l in these states are:

Cum-project cash flows, X_q^ϕ

	Down-state $(\phi = d)$	**Middle-state** $(\phi = m)$	**Up-state** $(\phi = u)$
h	\$60	\$210	\$300
l	\$0	\$30	\$300

The value of h's cash flows, $V_h^X = \$190$ and the value of l's cash flows, $V_l^X = \$110$.

Under this θ^x, hazard rate IA is first negative and then positive and the security issued is the one that maximizes h's financing-NPV. To identify this security, we graph the $NPV_h^C(F)$ of the pooled debt, pooled equity, and the pooled debt–equity contracts (at face value $b = \$30$).

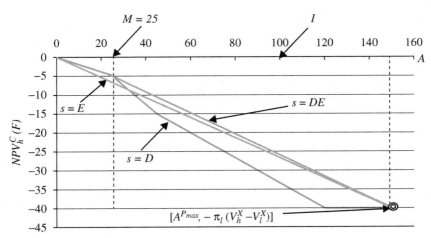

Hazard Rate *IA* First Negative then Positive

Consistent with Proposition 10a, debt maximizes h's financing-NPV when M is low (less than \$25) and debt–equity maximizes h's financing-NPV when M is high (greater than \$25).

9.3. Illustrating Results for Proposition 10c

We derive a second result that helps us understand the firm's financing policy where the sign of hazard rate *IA* changes. Firms with high risk and those for which a greater proportion of value *IA* comes from downside *IA* are more likely to choose a contract that contains equity (either with or without debt).

9.3.1. *Downside IA and Equity Issuance*

At t_0, the firm has no slack and an investment opportunity that will require $60. Thus, if it is to invest in the project, it must raise $60 in capital. There are two equi-probable states (u and d) next period. To see how downside *IA* affects the firm's financing choices, consider three cases — the Base case, Case 1, and Case 2 — each with a different amount of downside *IA*. The cum-project cash flows for h and l in each case are:

Cum-project cash flows, X_q^ϕ

	Base case		Case 1		Case 2	
	Down-state, d	Up-state, u	Down-state, d	Up-state, u	Down-state, d	Up-state, u
Firm h	$40	$320	$50	$310	$60	$300
Firm l	$20	$240	$10	$250	$0	$260

The value of h's and l's cash flows and value *IA* are the same for all three cases. Specifically, h's value is $180, l's is 130, and value *IA* is $180 - $130 = 50. There are two sources of value *IA* — downside *IA* and upside *IA*.

- In the base case, downside *IA* is $40 - $20 = 20, and upside *IA* is $320 - $240 = 80.
- In Case 1, downside *IA* is 40 and upside *IA* is 60.
- In Case 2, downside *IA* is 60 and upside *IA* is 40.

Thus, the proportion of value *IA* that comes from downside *IA* is the smallest for the base case and largest for Case 2.

We next examine the financing choices for each of the three cases. In each of these cases, θ^x is such that the sign of hazard rate IA changes and the security issued is the one that maximizes h's financing-NPV. To identify this security, we graph the $NPV_h^C(F)$ of the pooled debt, pooled equity, and the pooled debt–equity contracts.

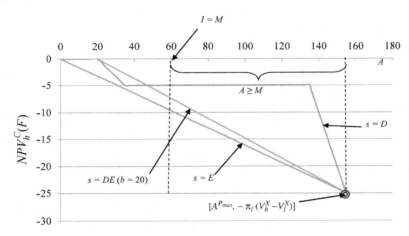

Downside IA: Base Case

In the base case, debt maximizes h's financing-NPV. The firm chooses a debt contract.

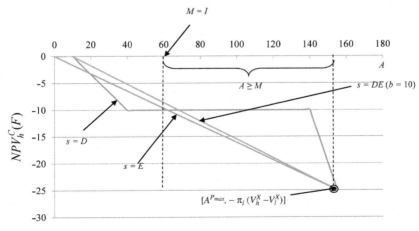

Downside IA: Case 1

In case 1, note that a debt–equity contract (with face value, $b = 10$) maximizes h's financing-NPV. The firm thus chooses a debt–equity contract.

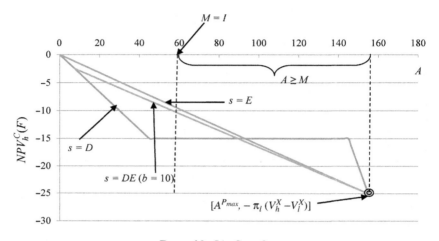

Downside *IA*: Case 2

In Case 2, note that equity contract maximizes h's financing-NPV. The firm thus chooses equity.

Taken collectively, the analysis in the three cases can be summarized as follows: as downside IA increases, the firm's financing choice changes from debt to equity, first as part of the debt–equity contract and then without any debt. That is, the likelihood of a contract with equity being chosen increases.

9.3.2. *Risk and Equity Issuance*

At t_0, the firm has no slack but has an investment opportunity that will require \$15. Thus, if it to invest in the project, it requires \$15 in capital. Assume now, that there are five equiprobable states and further, for simplicity, that the risk of the cash flows of each firm-type is the same. To see how risk affects financing choice, consider two cases of $t = 1$ cash flows — the

Base case and Case 1 — each with a different risk. The cash flows in each case are:

Cum-project cash flows, X_q^ϕ

	Base case					Case 1				
	State 1	State 2	State 3	State 4	State 5	State 1	State 2	State 3	State 4	State 5
Firm h	$25	$40	$70	$100	$115	$10	$20	$70	$120	$130
Firm l	$15	$30	$60	$90	$105	$0	$10	$60	$110	$120

The value of h's and l's cash flows and value IA are the same for both cases. Specifically, h's value is $70, l's is 60, and value IA is $70 - \$60 = \$10$. The volatility of cash flows for each firm-type in the base case is $34.21. The volatility of cash flows for each firm-type in Case 1 is $55.28. Thus, the risk of the cash flows under Case 1 is larger than the risk under the base case.

Using an analysis similar to the previous example, we examine, next, the firm's financing choice in each case.

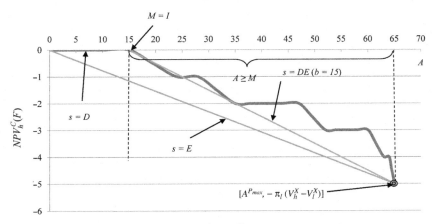

Risk : Base Case

In the base case, debt maximizes h's financing-NPV. The firm chooses a debt contract (in fact, the debt contract is risk-free).

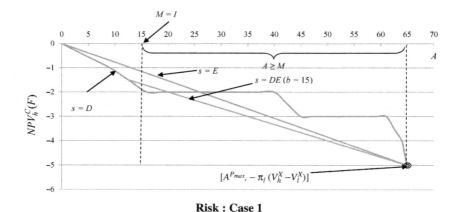

Risk : Case 1

Under Case 1, the firm issues an equity contract. Taken collectively, the analysis in the two cases shows that as risk increases, the firm's likelihood of issuing equity increases.

Chapter 10

Empirical Predictions and Implications for Practitioners: Debt–Equity Security Space

10.1. Financing Policy

In this chapter, we discuss the implications of Chapter 8 results for empiricists and practitioners. We begin with a discussion of financing policy. To bring out the significance of our findings, we place our findings in the context of results in the prior literature.

10.1.1. *Prior Research Findings*

The seminal Myers and Majluf (1984) analysis showed that when managers have private information about just the mean of the firm's future cash flows, financing policy follows a pecking order: in raising capital, a firm first prefers to issue the least risky security, then the second least risky security, and so on. This implies that if, for exogenous reasons, only debt and equity can be issued, the firm will always prefer debt over equity. Equity issuance cannot be rationalized. Based on this result, the extant research [e.g., Frank and Goyal (2003)] has argued that firms facing severe *IA*, such as small growth firms, should never issue equity. However, the empirical results are not consistent with this finding; researchers have found that equity issuance is particularly pervasive amongst small growth firms.

Other *IA* researchers have shown that equity issuance can be justified, but they have done so either in specific situations or by invoking other imperfections (in addition to *IA*). These papers thus cannot explain the observed pervasiveness of equity issuance. The next few paragraphs elaborate.

Heinkel (1982) and Brennan and Kraus (1987) have argued that when *IA* exists, equity is optimal only if it is accompanied by debt financing or redemption. However, this implication of their models cannot explain the findings in Hovakimian *et al.* (2004) that between 1982 and 2000 over 2,000 large equity issues (greater than 5% of total assets) were not accompanied by debt issues or redemption.

Axelson (2007) and Fulghieri and Lukin (2001) have justified equity issuance for initial public offerings (IPOs). Axelson (2007) rationalizes equity issuance by assuming that investors have private information before an IPO is issued. Fulghieri and Lukin (2001) argue that equity issuance can make economic sense if it results in greater information production during the IPO process than issuing debt. These models, however, cannot explain secondary equity offerings (SEOs) which, as Fama and French (2005) note, are an important source of financing.[1]

---

[1] They find that 30% of small firms and 40% of big firms do an SEO sometime during each 10-year period between 1973 and 2002.

Garcia *et al.* (2013) show that if a firm has multiple types of assets, equity issuance is optimal only when the asset with the lower value *IA* has higher risk; the asset with the higher value *IA* must have lower risk.

Finally, recent models [e.g., Morellec and Schürhoff (2011) and Hennessy *et al.* (2010)] have shown that when bankruptcy costs are invoked in addition to *IA*, equity issuance can be justified for small growth firms. However, the empirical evidence [e.g., Frank and Goyal (2003)] is that small-growth firms issue equity even after controlling for bankruptcy costs.

Thus, while existing research has found that equity issuance is optimal under certain specific situations, it cannot explain the observed widespread issuance of equity by a large cross section of firms. This may lead one to conclude that *IA* is not a first order effect on the firm's debt–equity choice. Our analysis, which has generalized assumptions regarding firm-specific variables, suggests that such a conclusion may be premature. We elaborate next.

10.1.2. *Our Findings*

When the lower-valued firm has lower credit risk (higher credit rating), *IA* is costless and when the lower-valued firm has higher credit risk, *IA* is costly. Regardless of whether *IA* is costless or costly, we find that:

Implication 1. Firms with higher risk and those for which a larger proportion of value *IA* comes from downside *IA*, are more likely to issue equity (either with or without debt).[2]

Label firms satisfying these *characteristics* as "equity-oriented firms". This finding is interesting for two reasons.

---

[2]Note from Table 2 (column III), there is a subtle distinction between the costless and costly *IA* cases.

First, in contrast to Myers–Majluf, equity issuance by firms with large *IA* about the mean/value of the firm's cash flows is optimal when a large proportion of their value *IA* is from the downside or they have higher risk.

Second, in contrast to existing research, equity issuance is optimal in many situations. In contrast to Heinkel (1982) and Brennan and Kraus (1987), we find that equity issuance is optimal even without the contemporaneous issuance of debt. In contrast to Axelson (2007) and Fulghieri and Lukin (2001), our model rationalizes equity issuance in both IPOs and SEOs because it is agnostic about whether the firm is public or private prior to raising capital. In contrast to Garcia *et al.*, our model shows that what matters is the total risk and thus equity issuance can be optimal even if the asset with the larger value *IA* has higher risk. Finally, in contrast to Morellec and Schürhoff (2011) and Hennessy *et al.* (2010), our model justifies equity issuance without relying on bankruptcy costs.

We next identify the kind of firms with greater risk and greater dependence on downside *IA* and show that this investigation yields additional implications.

(i) *Firms without credit ratings.* Ratings implicitly provide information about a firm's downside cash flows — it is these cash flows that determine the likelihood of default and the debtholders' payoffs in default. Consequently, firms that choose to subject themselves to the scrutiny of rating agencies are likely to have less downside *IA*; conversely, non-rated firms will likely have large downside *IA*. This insight, in conjunction with Implication 1 yields:

Implication 2. Firms without credit ratings are more likely to issue equity.

This implication is consistent with the findings in Tang (2009). Further, it reconciles the conflicting findings regarding credit ratings, debt capacity, and financing choice. Lemmon and Zender (2010) find that firms without credit agency-rated debt issue more equity. They suggest that this is because these firms have lower debt capacity than rated firms. However, Leary and Roberts (2006) find that debt capacity does not explain equity issuance by non-rated firms. Our model suggests that the Lemmon–Zender findings may be a consequence of unrated firms having higher downside IA and greater risk and not because of lower debt capacity.

(ii) *Small firms, and firms with high Tobin's q.* Prior research indicates that small, younger growth firms have greater risk and greater downside IA. Specifically, it has been argued that:

- Smaller and younger firms are less likely to be rated than larger and older firms [Lemmon and Zender (2010)]. From the discussion in (i), it follows that these firms are likely to have higher downside IA.
- Smaller firms have more risk [e.g., see Fama and French (1992)] and
- High growth (i.e., high Tobin's q) firms have higher downside IA [Axelson (2007)].

These points collectively, in conjunction with Implication 1, suggest:

Implication 3. Small and younger growth firms are more likely to issue equity.

This implication, which is consistent with the findings in Fama and French (2002) and Frank and Goyal (2003), is important for two reasons.

First, it explains some of the contradictory findings about a firm's debt–equity choice. Shyam-Sunder and Myers (1999) find that the financing behavior of the 157 firms that traded continuously over the period 1971–1989 conforms to the pecking order theory. Fama and French (2002) and Frank and Goyal (2003) find that the pecking order theory can describe the financing behavior of firms considered by Shyam-Sunder–Myers, but not for small growth firms. They find this puzzling because small, high-growth firms are often thought of as firms with greater IA. Our analysis suggests a potential explanation for these findings. Firms that traded continuously from 1971–1989 are older and hence are more likely to be evaluated by credit agencies [Lemmon and Zender (2010)]. They thus have lower credit risk spread, and are more likely to be debt-financed. However, small high-growth firms prefer equity because they have higher risk and/or have higher downside IA.

Second, the implication that high growth (i.e., high Tobin's q) firms are more likely to issue equity provides an IA-based explanation for the leverage results in some earlier studies. Baker and Wurgler (2002) found that high market-to-book firms have lower leverage ratios because they issue equity when raising new capital. They argue that this is evidence of market timing. Kayhan and Titman (2007), however, show that leverage ratios are affected not by the contemporaneous market-to-book ratios but by long-term average market-to-book ratios. They argue that the latter can proxy for growth opportunities. Our model, because it posits a positive relation between equity issuance and growth opportunities, advances an IA-based explanation for the observed negative relation between leverage and market-to-book ratios.

(iii) *Firms with more intangible assets.* Asset tangibility is an important determinant of the magnitude of the cash flows in the downside [e.g., in liquidation/reorganization] and intangible assets are more informationally-sensitive than tangible assets. Thus, firms with higher intangible assets will also have a larger downside IA. It is also well known that firms with more intangible assets are riskier than firms with more tangible assets [see e.g., Myers (2001)]. The aforementioned discussion implies that:

Implication 4. Firms with more intangible assets are likely to issue more equity.

This implication provides an *IA*-based explanation for the empirical evidence that firms with more intangible assets issue equity [see e.g., Titman and Wessels (1988)]. Prior *IA* research, following the pecking order theory, has argued that firms with intangible assets will have greater *IA* and are thus more likely to issue debt [Harris and Raviv (1991)]. Consequently, it is generally believed that the negative relationship between leverage and intangibility is because intangible assets are harder to collateralize and hence are associated with higher bankruptcy costs [see e.g., Frank and Goyal (2003)]. Our analysis suggests that even *IA* yields the same prediction.

(iv) *Firms that hedge less and are less diversified.* Firms that do not hedge and are not diversified will have higher risk. Thus,

Implication 5. Firms that do not hedge or are undiversified, issue more equity.

This implication is consistent with findings in Graham and Rogers (2002) and Comment and Jarrell (1995).

Implications 2–5 suggest that in a world of *IA*, equity oriented firms: (a) are small, (b) have a high Tobin's q ratio (growth firms), (c) are unrated by credit agencies, (d) have intangible assets, (e) are undiversified firms, and (f) hedge less.

Taken collectively, our analysis suggests that in a world where *IA* is the only imperfection, equity issuance is optimal for a wide cross-section of firms and in many situations.

10.2. Investment Policy

We again begin with a discussion of the findings of prior research.

10.2.1. *Prior Research Findings*

Myers and Majluf (1984) demonstrated that when the manager has private information, the lower-valued firm always invests in its positive-NPV project. However, the higher-valued firm will under-invest *iff* its cost of raising capital exceeds its project-NPV.

Such investment inefficiencies not only adversely affect a firm's competitive advantage, but reduce social welfare because of a reduction in employment etc. Myers and Majluf (1984) along with other researchers have attempted to identify mechanisms that can lower the cost of raising capital and hence lower the possibility of under-investment. The first mechanism is financing policy (i.e., the pecking order theory) and we have discussed this issue in detail earlier in this chapter. We now focus on some of the other mechanisms discussed in the extant research.

10.2.1.1. Reducing volatility of financing needs: Risk management

Froot *et al.* (1993) have argued that if the cost of raising capital are convex in the amount of capital raised,[3] hedging of macro risks in the period *prior* to raising capital — because

---

[3]This rationale for risk management only applies to firms with negative hazard rate *IA*. To see why, first note that this rationale requires *IA* costs to be convex. In Chapter 8, we demonstrated that equity costs are linear in the amount of capital raised. Thus for *IA* costs to be convex, the optimal security must be debt and, further, the cost of debt must be convex in capital raised. This only happens when hazard rate *IA* is negative.

it reduces the volatility of external capital needs — reduces *IA* costs.[4]

10.2.1.2. Altering financing needs: Corporate cash holdings and diversification mergers

Myers and Majluf (1984) demonstrate that firms can reduce the cost of raising capital by reducing its financing needs. One way to achieve that goal is to hold more cash (slack).

Myers–Majluf also argue that *IA* costs can be reduced if a firm with additional cash (slack) merges with a firm that has insufficient cash. This is because such mergers create internal markets in which the cash-rich firm can finance the projects of the cash-poor firm. This reduces the firm's total external financing needs in any given time period. One way to create such internal capital markets is through diversification mergers [see e.g., Akbulut and Matsusaka (2010)].

10.2.1.3. Expanding the security space: Issuing securities other than debt and equity

Historically, debt and equity were the only securities that the manager would consider issuing. One reason was that investors charge an "uncertainty premium" for holding an unfamiliar security [Gale (1992)]. By issuing standard securities such as debt and equity, firms avoid paying this cost. This does not mean that

---

[4]There are other *IA* models that also demonstrate the optimality of hedging macro risks. For example, in Breeden and Viswanathan (1998) firms hedge macro risks because it reduces *IA* about managerial quality and increases the compensation for high-quality managers. In DeMarzo and Duffie (1991) stockholders, because they cannot do it themselves, will want firms to hedge risks associated with private information. However, these arguments are not relevant to the issue being studied here — policies of a firm that must raise external capital to finance its investment opportunities.

new securities cannot be part of the security space. Gale (1992, p. 731) argues that if many firms want to issue a new security, investors may find it worthwhile to learn about the new securities since, by purchasing a large number of new securities, they can recoup the cost of becoming informed.

One reason why many firms may want to issue a security other than debt and equity is to reduce the cost of raising capital in the presence of imperfections such as *IA* [Tufano (2003)]. Several models have shown that expanding the security space to include securities such as warrants, and callable and convertible securities help reduce the cost of raising capital when there is *IA* between the manager and outsiders. They show that the costs reduce for a variety of reasons. For example, warrants, and callable and convertible securities allow managers to take advantage of public information revealed after the firm has raised capital [Chakraborty *et al.* (2011)] and promote better information production [Fulghieri and Lukin (2001)].

10.2.2. *Our Findings*

Like Myers–Majluf, we find that the higher-valued firm will under-invest when its cost of raising capital exceeds its project-*NPV*. We further find that such under-investment is only an issue for firms whose credit risk *IA* is negative. Our analysis suggests at least three ways to reduce the cost of raising capital and hence the possibility of under-investment. Two of these approaches are novel.

10.2.2.1. Reducing risk: Risk management and diversification

The first approach involves altering θ^x. Note from Table 2 that *IA* costs can be reduced by lowering the firm's credit risk spread and/or value *IA*. One way to accomplish this goal is to provide private information to the market. For example, the firm can reduce credit risk spread by providing more information to credit agencies. However, as is well known, disclosing private information can erode the firm's competitive advantage. There is another way.

Implication 6. When the manager raises capital, he can lower his costs by *simultaneously* entering into risk-management (operational or financial hedging) contracts or a diversifying merger.

The reasoning is straight-forward. Reducing the risk of the firm's cash flows reduces credit risk spread (Propositions 10c and 11c), and thereby the cost of raising capital. As discussed, "risk" refers to the volatility common to both firm-types.

To better understand what we mean here by risk and how such a risk can be reduced, consider an airline company whose revenues come from ticketing proceeds and costs from labor and fuel. The manager has private information about ticketing and labor costs and thus the magnitude of these costs depends on firm-type. However, fuel costs are the same for both firm-types. Thus, the volatility of fuel cost affects the risk of both firm-types. If the manager can reduce the volatility of firm's overall cash flows by, for example, entering into forward/future oil contracts or a diversifying merger (e.g., purchasing an oil company), he can reduce the firm's cost of raising capital.

Note that the role of risk-management and diversification mergers in our model is different from that in prior research. As discussed, prior research has argued that risk management and diversifying mergers must be undertaken in the period *prior* to raising capital (i.e., at $t = -1$) and that they reduce the cost of raising capital by altering the firm's financing needs.

10.2.2.2. Expanding the security space to complete markets

The second approach involves expanding the security space, S. Table 1 shows that IA is costlessly resolved when there is both a contract with $NPV_h^C(F) = 0$ and $NPV_l^C(F) \leq 0$, and a contract with $NPV_l^C(F) = 0$ and $NPV_h^C(F) \leq 0$. This condition is satisfied for all firms when the security space contains admissible securities that complete the markets (the proof of Proposition 12 shows this). Further, note from Table 1 that financing policy is partially irrelevant when IA is costless. Summarizing,

Proposition 12. When S is expanded to include admissible securities that complete the markets, IA becomes costless for all firms. Yet, financing policy is only partially irrelevant.

Proof. See Appendix.

Proposition 12 suggests that financial innovation that completes the markets will completely eliminate IA costs. This will, in turn, eliminate market inefficiencies and hence increase social welfare. It is important to note that corporate financing policy will *not* become irrelevant; it will be only partially irrelevant.

Proposition 12 raises an important question. What are the admissible securities that can help complete the markets? Some examples of such admissible securities include warrants, and callable and convertible securities. These securities are essentially options and, as is well known, options complete the markets.

Implication 7. Securities such as warrants, and callable and convertible securities, because they complete the markets, can reduce IA costs.

Earlier models that have shown that securities such as warrants can eliminate the cost of raising capital have relied on different arguments, as discussed previously.

10.2.2.3. Corporate cash holdings

The third approach involves altering the firm's financing needs. Table 2 shows that the cost of raising capital can be reduced by building up slack and reducing the firm's financing needs. As discussed, this idea is not novel; it was first proposed in the seminal Myers–Majluf analysis. These authors, however, do not explicitly identify the kinds of firms that will have higher cash holdings. In this regard, note that the greater the financing cost, the greater is the benefit to holding slack. In our model, h's losses are higher for firms with higher credit risk spread (Table 2) and, as seen, these are equity-oriented firms. Thus,

Implication 8. Managers of equity-oriented firms will hold more cash.

This implication is consistent with the evidence in Opler *et al.* (1999) who find that firms with higher cash holdings (i) are small, (ii) are high-growth, (iii) are in industries with high volatility of cash flows, (iv) have high volatility of firm-specific cash flows, (v) are unrated, and (vi) have high R&D investment (and thus greater intangible assets).

10.3. Market Reaction to Firm Policies: Announcement Period Returns

Jung *et al.* (1996) argue that a theory that explains a firm's capital-raising decisions should also explain how the markets react to these choices. In this context, it is well known that the markets react to capital-raising decisions only if a separating equilibrium occurs [Hennessy *et al.* (2010)]. Thus, by examining the situations in which a separating equilibrium occurs, the market's reaction to these choices can be assessed. In our framework, a separating equilibrium occurs both when credit risk IA is negative and when it is non-negative. Consider each case separately.

10.3.1. *Credit risk IA is non-negative*

As seen, the firm, regardless of its type accepts a contract. Thus, when the manager announces that he will raise financing (regardless of the security raised), his firm-type is not revealed to the markets and there is no market reaction. Further, if the manager issues equity, his firm-type is revealed to be l. The announcement of equity-financing will therefore generate lower returns than the announcement of debt issuance.

10.3.2. *Credit risk IA is negative*

When the manager announces his decision to raise financing (regardless of the security issued), stock returns are lower when h's financing cost is higher (this increases the likelihood that h will under-invest and l will be the only firm-type raising capital). As seen, our analysis suggests that equity-oriented firms suffer from greater financing costs. Thus, stock returns are lower for such firms than for debt-oriented firms (i.e., firms for which debt is optimal). Further, among equity-oriented firms, announcement returns will be higher when equity is issued than when debt is issued. This is because, for these firms, equity is the security that minimizes h's loss. This implies that a firm that issues debt must be l (see the earlier discussion of financing polices).

Implication 9. Announcement period returns: (i) are larger, on average, for debt and (ii) for equity oriented firms, are larger under equity financing.

Implication 9(i) is consistent with the results in the Myers–Majluf model and with the findings in several empirical studies [see Frank and Goyal's (2005) survey]. However, Implication 9(ii) contrasts with the Myers–Majluf model which argues that announcement period returns should be larger for *all* firms under debt financing. Our analysis suggests that returns for equity-oriented firms — which include high Tobin's q firms, small firms, firms with intangible assets, firms without credit ratings, and undiversified and less hedged firms — will be higher under equity financing. The implication regarding announcement period returns for high Tobin's q firms is consistent with Jung *et al.* (1996) who find that when equity is issued, the announcement returns for these firms are larger. The implications for announcement period returns for the remaining equity-oriented firms (e.g., firms unrated by credit agencies) are yet to be tested.

Chapter 11

Concluding Remarks

A firm's investment and financing policies and its cost of raising capital depend on firm characteristics (the nature of the manager's private information and the firm's financing needs) and on the assumed security space (S). This means that the firm's policies and costs are sensitive to alternative assumptions about firm characteristics and the set of securities that the manager is assumed to be able to issue.

There is thus a logical imperative. To fully understand the implications of IA it is necessary to derive a theory that applies to *all* firms in the economy (i.e., without making any assumptions about firm characteristics) and under *any* assumption regarding S.

This book accomplishes this goal. Our generalization, as seen, overturns some existing insights and yields new theoretical results that are largely consistent with prior empirical findings. In addition, it also yields several insights for practitioners.

There at least three potential directions for future research. The first pertains to capital structure theory. Frank and Goyal (2005) call for a unifying model that can explain 17 stylized empirical facts that they identify. It is unlikely that a model in which *IA* is the only "imperfection" can explain all of these empirical facts. A useful unifying model will likely require a theory that incorporates elements of at least two of the main competing capital structure models — the tradeoff and *IA*-based theories. Myers (1984) contains an insight regarding how such a unifying model can be built. He suggests that one begin with a "generalized *IA* theory" and then incorporate elements of the static tradeoff theory that find empirical support.

By generalizing firm characteristics and the security space our paper has taken an important step towards such a generalized *IA* theory. It would be useful for future theoretical research to generalize the *IA* theory even further by relaxing two of our model assumptions, namely, our assumptions about the static nature of *IA* and our exogenous specification of the manager's objective function. Relaxing the first of these assumptions [along the lines in e.g., Fulghieri and Lukin (2001)] can improve our understanding of how *IA* affects firm choices in a dynamic environment. Relaxing the second, that is, endogenizing the manager's objective function [as in e.g., Dybvig and Zender (1991)], can help us understand how firms can design managerial contracts to minimize the cost of raising capital, and thereby reduce investment inefficiencies.

A second research avenue relates to empirical research. We have argued that a wide cross-section of firms (which include small firms, high Tobin's q firms (growth firms), firms that are unrated by credit agencies, firms with intangible assets, and firms that are undiversified and those that do not use hedging) issue equity. Further, we have argued that these firms will also hold more cash and that they will experience higher stock returns when they issue equity (rather than debt). These implications are largely consistent with the findings in the empirical research.

However, we recognize that other market frictions, most notably bankruptcy costs, also yield similar predictions. This is because more risky firms have a higher cost of debt both according to our model and in the presence of bankruptcy costs. Therefore, as a next step, it is important to determine if our results are an implication of *IA* between managers and outsiders or of other market frictions.

While such an empirical analysis is clearly outside the scope of the present analysis, we offer some suggestions about how such tests can be conducted. Specifically, we suggest that researchers first form portfolios of similar firms, with the first portfolio containing the most equity-oriented firms and the last containing the least equity-oriented firms. Then, controlling for other market frictions such as bankruptcy costs, they can determine if the firm's financing behavior can be explained by the theory or by the other market imperfections.

A third research avenue pertains to the question of the existence of equilibrium in screening models. In contrast to Rothschild and Stiglitz's (1976) wherein an equilibrium may not exist, we have shown that a unique equilibrium will always exist in our generalized capital-raising model. We believe that a more formal investigation of why equilibrium exists in our model will be a fruitful endeavor.

Part V

Appendix

This Appendix provides the proofs for our propositions. For the reader's convenience, we also restate the propositions before proving them.

Proposition 1. The proposition states that investors offer all contracts with (i) $s \in S$, (ii) $A \geq M$, and (iii) $NPV_q^C(F) = 0$. Further, it states that the manager picks any one of the offered $NPV_q^C(F) = 0$ contracts randomly.

Proof. Once offered all $NPV_q^C(F) = 0$ contracts, the manager's decision is straightforward and needs no explanation. Further, it is easy to see that the investors can only offer contracts with $A \geq M$, and $s \in S$. To prove that investors will offer all $NPV_q^C(F) = 0$ and no other contracts, it is sufficient to show that: (i) investors will not offer any $NPV_q^C(F) < 0$ or $NPV_q^C(F) > 0$ contract and (ii) it is optimal for the investor to offer all $NPV_q^C(F) = 0$ contracts.

Part I: Investors will not offer any $NPV_q^C(F) < 0$ or $NPV_q^C(F) > 0$ contract. Consider each contract separately.

(i) *A $NPV_q^C(F) < 0$ contract.* Suppose both investors — 1 and 2 — offer a contract set containing such a contract C with terms $[A, s, \vec{P_s}]$.[1] Two possibilities arise. In each case, the investor will not offer the contract. This is because either the contract is redundant or because there is another contract that will yield higher profits for the investor.

(a) *C is optimal for q.* The firm will pick contract C from any investor at random. The probability that the contract is chosen from any particular investor is 0.5 and each investor's expected profit is $-0.5NPV_q^C(F) > 0$. Suppose that investor 1 deviates and offers C' with terms $[A + \varepsilon, s, \vec{P_s}]$. This is the same contract as C but with ε more capital. Investor 2 continues to offer C. Firm q will pick C' since $NPV_q^{C'}(F) = NPV_q^C(F) + \varepsilon > NPV_q^C(F)$. Now, investor 1's profits are $-NPV_q^{C'}(F) = -NPV_q^C(F) - \varepsilon$. If ε is sufficiently small, investor 1 earns a higher profit by offering C'.

(b) *C is not optimal for q.* The contract is redundant.

The investor will therefore not offer this contract.

(ii) *A $NPV_q^C(F) > 0$ contract.* Again, suppose both investors offer a contract set containing a $NPV_q^C(F) > 0$ contract C with terms $[A, s, \vec{P_s}]$. Two possibilities arise. In each, either the contract is redundant or there is another contract that will yield higher profits for the investor.

(a) *C is optimal for q.* Each investor's profit is $-0.5NPV_q^C(F) < 0$. Investors are better off not offering this contract (they will earn zero profits).

(b) *C is not optimal for q.* The contract is redundant.

---

[1]In the proofs of many propositions like this one, we demonstrate that a particular contract $C = [A, s, \vec{P_s}]$ cannot be offered. To prove this, we first assume that *both* investors offer the contract and then show that it is not consistent with optimizing behavior. However, the proofs go through even if *one* investor offers such a contract.

The investor will therefore not offer this contract. The only contracts that the investor may offer are $NPV_q^C(F) = 0$ contracts.

Part II: Investors will offer all $NPV_q^C(F) = 0$ contracts. Investors' expected profits are zero regardless of whether they offer no contract, one, or all $NPV_q^C(F) = 0$ contracts [Eq. (6b)]. In equilibrium, investors offer the largest set, i.e., they will offer all $NPV_q^C(F) = 0$ contracts.

Proposition 2. This proposition states that a firm can have any capital structure after it raises capital.

Proof. To prove this proposition it is sufficient to show that the manager can issue any security and raise any amount of capital, A, up to and including the cum-project value of V_q^X.

The manager can pick any contract with $NPV_q^C(F) = 0$, i.e., any contract with $A = V_q^s(\vec{P}_s)$. Since each security, s, is admissible, there exists at least one $\vec{P}_s$, for every $V_q^s(\vec{P}_s)$ up to and including V_q^X. The previous two statements together imply that the manager can raise any $A \leq V_q^X$ with any security.

Proposition 3. This propostion states that the investor will only offer pooled and no-loss contracts for which $A \geq M$ and $s \in S$.

Proof. It is easy to see that the investor can only offer contracts with $A \geq M$ and $s \in S$. What remains to be shown is that investors will only offer pooled and no-loss contracts.

All $A \geq M$ and $s \in S$ contracts can be divided into five mutually exclusive yet exhaustive categories:

(i) $\sum_q \pi_q NPV_q^C(F) < 0$ contracts with $NPV_h^C(F) < 0$ and $NPV_l^C(F) > 0$,

(ii) $\sum_q \pi_q NPV_q^C(F) < 0$ contracts with $NPV_h^C(F) > 0$ and $NPV_l^C(F) < 0$,

(iii) $\sum_q \pi_q NPV_q^C(F) < 0$ contracts with $NPV_h^C(F) < 0$ and $NPV_l^C(F) < 0$,

(iv) $\sum_q \pi_q NPV_q^C(F) > 0$ contracts, and

(v) pooled and no-loss contracts.

To prove this proposition it is sufficient to show that investors cannot offer any contracts in categories (i)–(iv). Consider, first, the contracts in category (i).

(i) **$A \sum_q \pi_q NPV_q^C(F) < 0$ contract with $NPV_h^C(F) < 0$ and $NPV_l^C(F) > 0$.** Suppose that both investors — 1 and 2 — offer a contract set containing such a contract, C. This contract is described by $[A, s, \vec{P_s}]$. Four possibilities arise. In each, either the contract is redundant or there is another contract that will yield higher profits for the investor.

(a) *C is optimal for both h and l.* The firm will pick C from any investor at random. The probability that the contract is chosen from any particular investor is 0.5 and each investor's profit is $-0.5 \sum_q \pi_q NPV_q^C(F) > 0$. Suppose that investor 1 deviates to offer C' with terms $[A + \varepsilon, s, \vec{P_s}]$. This is the same contract as C but with ε more capital. Investor 2 continues to offer C. Each firm-type will pick C' since $NPV_q^{C'}(F) = NPV_q^C(F) + \varepsilon > NPV_q^C(F)$. Now, investor 1's profit is $-\sum_q \pi_q NPV_q^{C'}(F) = -\sum_q \pi_q NPV_q^C(F) - \varepsilon$. If ε is sufficiently small, investor 1's profit is higher by offering C'.

(b) *C is optimal only for h.* Suppose l picks another offered contract, say C'''. For simplicity, assume this contract is offered by both investors. Each investor's profit is $-0.5[\pi_h NPV_h^C(F) + \pi_l NPV_l^{C'''}(F)]$. Suppose investor 1 deviates and offers C', that is described by $[A + \varepsilon, s, \vec{P_s}]$ where $\varepsilon \to 0$. Now, h picks C' but l continues to pick C'' since ε is small. Now, investor 1's profits are $-\pi_h NPV_h^{C'}(F) - 0.5[\pi_l NPV_l^{C''}(F)] = -\pi_h[NPV_h^C(F) + \varepsilon] - 0.5[\pi_l NPV_l^{C''}(F)]$. Since ε is sufficiently small, investor 1 earns a higher expected profit by offering C'.

(c) *C is optimal only for l.* Suppose h picks C'' which is offered by both investors. Each investor's profit is $-0.5[\pi_h NPV_h^{C''}(F) + \pi_l NPV_l^C(F)]$. Suppose investor 1 deviates by not offering C; investor 2 continues to offer C. Now, l will pick C from investor 2 and h will pick C'' from any investor. Investor 1's profits are $-0.5\pi_h NPV_h^{C''}(F)$. Since $NPV_l^C(F) > 0$, investor 1's profits are higher by not offering C.

(d) *C is not optimal for h or l.* The contract is redundant.

Thus, the investor will not offer such contracts. A similar analysis demonstrates that investors will not offer contracts in categories (ii)–(iv). Thus, the only contracts that can be offered are pooled and no-loss contracts.

Proposition 4. This proposition states that the candidate contracts set, $\Omega^C[\theta^x, M, S]$, has only one of two compositions. Under the first, $NPV_h^C(F) < 0$ for all contracts [$NPV_l^C(F) \geq 0$ under these contracts.] Under the second, there also exists a contract with $NPV_h^C(F) = 0$ and $NPV_l^C(F) \leq 0$.

Proof. This proof has two parts. The first part shows that the financing-*NPV*s of the contracts in the candidate contracts set must satisfy four conditions. The second shows that only the two aforementioned compositions satisfy these four conditions. Throughout this proof, assume that an admissible security, s, is defined by n parameters: $p_s^1 \ldots p_s^n$. Without loss of generality, $V_l^s(\vec{P}_s)$ is increasing in parameters $p_s^1 \ldots p_s^m$ and decreasing in $p_s^{m+1} \ldots p_s^n$ where $0 \leq m \leq n$. Admissible security property 4 implies that $V_h^s(\vec{P}_s)$ is also increasing in parameters $p_s^1 \dots p_s^m$ and decreasing in $p_s^{m+1} \dots p_s^n$.

Part I: Financing-NPVs of contracts in $\Omega^C[\theta^x, M, S]$ must satisfy four conditions. A contract is a pooled contract if $A = \sum_q \pi_q V_q^s(\vec{P}_s)$. Based on financing-*NPV*s, a pooled contract is one of three types: a pooled $C1$ contract if $NPV_h^C(F) > 0$ and $NPV_l^C(F) < 0$ under the contract, a pooled $C2$ contract if $NPV_h^C(F) < 0$ and $NPV_l^C(F) > 0$, and a pooled $C3$ contract if $NPV_h^C(F) = NPV_l^C(F) = 0$. Similarly, a contract is no-loss contract if $A = Min\left[V_h^s(\vec{P}_s), V_l^s(\vec{P}_s)\right]$. Each no-loss contract is one of two types: a no-loss $C4$ contract if $NPV_h^C(F) = 0$ and $NPV_l^C(F) < 0$ and a no-loss $C5$ contract if $NPV_h^C(F) < 0$ and $NPV_l^C(F) = 0$.

The properties of admissible securities and $V_h^X > V_l^X$ imply that the financing-*NPV*s of contracts in $\Omega^C[\theta^x, M, S]$ satisfy the four requirements mentioned in the following paragraphs.

(i) $\Omega^C[\theta^x, M, S]$ *always contains a pooled $C2$ and a no-loss $C5$ contract.* A pooled (no-loss) contract C with terms $[A, s, \vec{P}_s]$ is in $\Omega^C[\theta^x, M, S]$, if $A \geq M$. Further, it is of type $C2$ $(C5)$ if $V_h^s(\vec{P}_s) - V_l^s(\vec{P}_s) > 0$ [see Eqs. (12a)–(12b) and (13a)–(13c)]. To prove this requirement, it is thus sufficient to show that there exists at least one pooled and at least one no-loss contract with $A \geq M$ and $V_h^s(\vec{P}_s) - V_l^s(\vec{P}_s) > 0$.

Admissible Properties 2 and 4 imply that for an admissible security s, there must exist a $\vec{P}_s$ for which $V_q^s(\vec{P}_s) = V_q^X \forall q$. For this $(s, \vec{P}_s)$, a pooled contract provides $A = \sum_q \pi_q V_q^X$ [Eq. (8)] and a no-loss contract provides $A = V_l^X$ [Eq. (10a)]. Since, by assumption, $NPV_q(I) > 0$ and $X_q^\phi(FA) > 0$, it follows that $V_q^X \equiv V_q^X(FA) + V_q^X(I) > I \geq M \forall q$. Thus, at $(s, \vec{P}_s)$, pooled contracts provide $A = \sum_q \pi_q V_q^X > M$ and no-loss contracts provide $A = min\left[V_h^X, V_l^X\right] = V_l^X > M$ $[V_h^X > V_l^X > M$

by assumption]. Further, $V_h^s(\vec{P}_s) - V_l^s(\vec{P}_s) = V_h^X - V_l^X > 0$. Thus, there exists at least one pooled and at least one no-loss contract with $A \geq M$ and $V_h^s(\vec{P}_s) - V_l^s(\vec{P}_s) > 0$.

(ii) *If* $\Omega^C[\theta^x, M, S]$ *contains a pooled* $C1$ *contract it also contains a pooled* $C3$ *contract.* A pooled contract, $[A', s, \vec{P}_s']$, is of type $C1$ if $V_h^s(\vec{P}_s') - V_l^s(\vec{P}_s') < 0$ and it belongs to $\Omega^C[\theta^x, M, S]$ if $A' \geq M$. A pooled contract, $[A'', s, \vec{P}_s'']$, is of type $C3$ if $V_h^s(\vec{P}_s'') - V_l^s(\vec{P}_s'') = 0$ and it belongs to $\Omega^C[\theta^x, M, S]$ if $A'' \geq M$. To prove this requirement, it is thus sufficient to show that (a) the existence of a pooled $C1$ contract, $[A', s, \vec{P}_s']$ implies existence of a pooled $C3$ contract, $[A'', s, \vec{P}_s'']$ and (b) if $A' \geq M$ then $A'' \geq M$.

(a) *Existence of a pooled* $C1$ *contract implies existence of a pooled* $C3$ *contract.* A pooled $C1$ contract has $V_h^s(\vec{P}_s') - V_l^s(\vec{P}_s') < 0$. Since $V_q^s(\vec{P}_s)$ is continuous in p_s (admissible security property 2) so is $V_h^s(\vec{P}_s) - V_l^s(\vec{P}_s)$. Thus, increasing $p_s^1 \ldots p_s^m$ and/or decreasing $p_s^{m+1} \ldots p_s^n$ from $\vec{P}_s'$ must first yield a $\vec{P}_s''$ for which $V_h^s(\vec{P}_s'') - V_l^s(\vec{P}_s'') = 0$ and only then will there exist a $\vec{P}_s$ at which a pooled contract has $V_h^s(\vec{P}_s) - V_l^s(\vec{P}_s) > 0$ (this contract exists as seen in part (i)). Hence, the existence of a pooled $C1$ contract implies that there also is a pooled $C3$ contract under which $V_h^s(\vec{P}_s'') - V_l^s(\vec{P}_s'') = 0$.

(b) *If* $A' \geq M$ *then* $A'' \geq M$. Increasing $p_s^1 \ldots p_s^m$ and/or decreasing $p_s^{m+1} \ldots p_s^n$ from $\vec{P}_s'$ yields $\vec{P}_s''$ (see (a)). Further, both $V_l^s(\vec{P}_s)$ and $V_h^s(\vec{P}_s)$ are increasing in parameters $p_s^1 \ldots p_s^m$ and decreasing in $p_s^{m+1} \ldots p_s^n$. The previous two statements imply that $V_q^s(\vec{P}_s'') > V_q^s(\vec{P}_s') \forall q$. This means that the amount of capital under the $C3$ contract, $A'' = \sum_q \pi_q V_q^s(\vec{P}_s'') > \sum_q \pi_q V_q^s(\vec{P}_s') = A'$. Thus, if $A' \geq M$ then $A'' \geq M$.

Thus, if $\Omega^C[\theta^x, M, S]$ contains a pooled $C1$ contract, it will contain a pooled $C3$ contract.

(iii) *If $\Omega^C[\theta^x, M, S]$ contains a no-loss $C4$ contract it also contains a pooled $C1$ contract.* To prove this requirement, it is sufficient to show that the existence of a no-loss $C4$ contract, $[A', s, \vec{P}'_s]$, with $A' \geq M$ implies that, under the same $(s, \vec{P}'_s)$, a pooled contract, $[A, s, \vec{P}'_s]$, exists that (a) is of type $C1$ and (b) has $A \geq M$.

   (a) *Pooled contract is of type $C1$.* Since the no-loss contract is of type $C4$, $(s, \vec{P}'_s)$ must be such $V^s_h(\vec{P}'_s) - V^s_l(\vec{P}'_s) < 0$. Thus, under the same $(s, \vec{P}'_s)$, the pooled contract must also have $V^s_h(\vec{P}'_s) - V^s_l(\vec{P}'_s) < 0$. By definition, such a pooled contract is of type $C1$.

   (b) *Pooled contract has $A \geq M$.* Under the same $(s, \vec{P}'_s)$, the capital provided under pooled contract, $A = \sum_q \pi_q V^s_q(\vec{P}'_s)$ exceeds the capital under the no-loss contract $A' = Min[V^s_h(\vec{P}'_s), V^s_l(\vec{P}'_s)]$. Since $A' \geq M$, it follows that $A \geq M$.

   Thus, if a no-loss $C4$ contract exists in $\Omega^C[\theta^x, M, S]$, so does a pooled $C1$ contract.

(iv) *If $\Omega^C[\theta^x, M, S]$ contains a pooled $C1$ contract it also contains a no-loss $C4$ contract.* As seen in Part (ii), the existence of a pooled $C1$ contract $[A', s, \vec{P}'_s]$ implies that there exists a pooled $C3$ contract, $[A'', s, \vec{P}''_s]$. Here, $\vec{P}''_s$ has higher $p^1_s \dots p^m_s$ and/or lower $p^{m+1}_s \dots p^n_s$ than $\vec{P}'_s$, $V^s_q(\vec{P}''_s) > V^s_q(\vec{P}'_s) \forall q$, and $V^s_h(\vec{P}''_s) - V^s_l(\vec{P}''_s) = 0$. Further, $A'' = \sum_q \pi_q V^s_q(\vec{P}''_s) = V^s_h(\vec{P}''_s) > A' \geq M$. To prove the requirement here, it is thus sufficient to show that the existence of the pooled $C3$ contract, in turn, implies the existence of a no-loss $C4$ contract with $A \geq M$.

Under the pooled $C3$ contract $V_h^s(\vec{P}_s'') - V_l^s(\vec{P}_s'') = 0$. Consider a $\vec{P}_s$ with an $\varepsilon \to 0$ lower $p_s^1 \ldots p_s^m$ and/or $\varepsilon \to 0$ higher $p_s^{m+1} \ldots p_s^n$ than $\vec{P}_s''$. At this $\vec{P}_s$, a no-loss contract has $V_h^s(\vec{P}_s) - V_l^s(\vec{P}_s) < 0$ and thus will be of type $C4$. Further, the amount of capital under this no-loss contract, $A = Min[V_h^s(\vec{P}_s), V_l^s(\vec{P}_s)] = V_h^s(\vec{P}_s)$. If ε is small, $A = V_h^s(\vec{P}_s)$ is approximately equal to $A'' = V_h^s(\vec{P}_s'')$ and greater than A'. Thus $A \geq M$.

Thus, the existence of a pooled $C1$ contract implies the existence of a no-loss $C4$ contract, $[A, s, \vec{P}_s]$, with $A \geq M$.

Part II: Only two compositions satisfy the four afore-mentioned conditions. This part shows that only the two compositions in Proposition 4 satisfy the four aforestated conditions.

As noted, each pooled contracts is one of three types and each no-loss contracts is one of two types. This means that, based on financing-*NPV*s, each contract in $\Omega^C[\theta^x, M, S]$ is one of five-types. Simple combinatorial analysis yields that the contracts in $\Omega^C[\theta^x, M, S]$ collectively satisfy one of $2^5 = 32$ possibilities. Of these, it is easily verified that there are only three possibilities that also satisfy the four earlier-mentioned conditions. The first possibility is that $\Omega^C[\theta^x, M, S]$ contains only pooled $C2$ and no-loss $C5$ contracts. The second possibility is that $\Omega^C[\theta^x, M, S]$ contains (at least) one of each of the five-types of contracts. The third possibility is that $\Omega^C[\theta^x, M, S]$ contains only pooled $C2$, pooled $C3$, and no-loss $C5$ contracts.

In the first possibility, $\Omega^C[\theta^x, M, S]$ contains only contracts with $NPV_h^C(F) < 0$ and $NPV_l^C(F) \geq 0$. In the last two possibilities $\Omega^C[\theta^x, M, S]$ additionally contains a contract with $NPV_h^C(F) = 0$ and $NPV_l^C(F) \leq 0$.

Thus, the candidate contracts set has one of two mutually exclusive yet exhaustive compositions.

Proposition 5a. This proposition describes the equilibrium contracts set and the manager's decisions when $\Omega^C[\theta^x, M, S]$ contains only pooled contracts with $NPV_h^C(F) < 0$ and $NPV_l^C(F) > 0$ and no-loss contracts with $NPV_l^C(F) = 0$ and $NPV_h^C(F) < 0$ (composition 1). It states that when $C_h^{P_{max}}$ contract is economically viable for h, investors offer and the manager accepts the $C_h^{P_{max}}$ contract. When the $C_h^{P_{max}}$ contract is not viable for h, investors offer all no-loss contracts. The manager of firm l picks any offered contract; the manager of h rejects all contracts.

Proof. Consider the two cases — $C_h^{P_{max}}$ is viable, and $C_h^{P_{max}}$ is not viable — separately.

(i) $\boldsymbol{C_h^{P_{max}}}$ ***is viable for*** $\boldsymbol{h}$. The proof has four parts. The first part shows that, when offered the $C_h^{P_{max}}$ contract, it is optimal for the managers of both firm-types to accept the contract. The remaining three parts show that, in equilibrium, investors offer *only* the $C_h^{P_{max}}$ contract. The second part shows that h's financing-*NPV*, evaluated over all $\Omega^C[\theta^x, M, S]$ contracts, is maximized under the $C_h^{P_{max}}$ contract and l's financing-*NPV* among pooled contracts is minimized under $C_h^{P_{max}}$. Using this result, the third part shows that, in equilibrium, investors offer the $C_h^{P_{max}}$ contract. The fourth part demonstrates the uniqueness of this equilibrium by showing that no other contracts will be offered in equilibrium.

Part I: Manager's Decisions. Both investors offer the $C_h^{P_{max}}$ contract. The manager's only choice is either to accept the contract or reject it and not invest in the project. The manager will accept the contract if it is economically viable. Here $C_h^{P_{max}}$ is viable for h. Also, l gains under all pooled contracts in this composition, including $C_h^{P_{max}}$. This means that $C_h^{P_{max}}$ is viable for l too. Thus, the manager of both firm-types accept the contract.

Part II: Financing-NPVs of h and l under the $C_h^{P_{max}}$ contract. Under any $(s, \vec{P}')$, the capital provided under pooled contract, $A = \sum_q \pi_q V_q^s(\vec{P}'_s)$ exceeds the capital under the no-loss contract $A' = Min[V_h^s(\vec{P}'_s), V_l^s(\vec{P}'_s)]$. This means that h's financing-*NPV* is higher under a pooled contract. Thus, h's financing-*NPV* is maximized under the pooled contract with the highest $NPV_h^C(F)$, i.e., the $C_h^{P_{max}}$ contract.

For pooled contracts, $\sum_q \pi_q NPV_q^C(F) = 0$. Thus, among pooled contracts, l's financing-*NPV* is minimized under $C_h^{P_{max}}$.

Part III: Equilibrium Contracts Set contains the $C_h^{P_{max}}$ contract. The equilibrium contracts set contains this contract if no investor can deviate and earn higher profits by offering another contract C with $A \geq M$ and $s \in S$.

First, examine the conditions under which the investor can earn a higher profit. Suppose that both investors offer the $C_h^{P_{max}}$ contract. Since both firm-types will accept this contract (see Part I), investor profits are zero. To earn higher (positive) profits, as in Rothschild and Stiglitz (1976), an investor must offer a contract C that h would accept but l will not. This happens only if contract C satisfies each of the following conditions: $NPV_h^C(F) > NPV_h^{C_h^{P_{max}}}(F)$ and $NPV_l^C(F) < NPV_l^{C_h^{P_{max}}}(F)$.

All contracts C with $A \geq M$ can be placed into four groups as stated in the following points. Thus, to prove that no investor will deviate, it is sufficient to show that no contract in any of these groups satisfies the aforestated conditions.

(a) *Contract C with terms $[A, s, \vec{P}_s]$ under which $\sum_q \pi_q V_q^s$ $(\vec{P}_s) \geq M$ and $A = \sum_q \pi_q V_q^s(\vec{P}_s)$. These are the pooled contracts in $\Omega^C[\theta^x, M, S]$ that are other than $C_h^{P_{max}}$. For each, by definition, $NPV_h^C(F) < NPV_h^{C_h^{P_{max}}}(F)$. Thus, at least one of the conditions is not satisfied.*

(b) *Contract C with terms $[A, s, \vec{P}_s]$ under which $\sum_q \pi_q V_q^s$ $(\vec{P}_s) \geq M$ and $A > \sum_q \pi_q V_q^s(\vec{P}_s)$. These are contracts similar to pooled contracts in $\Omega^C[\theta^x, M, S]$ but with higher capital. Since l's financing-NPV for each pooled contract in $\Omega^C[\theta^x, M, S]$ exceeds $NPV_l^{C_h^{P_{max}}}(F)$, it follows that $NPV_l^C(F) > NPV_l^{C_h^{P_{max}}}(F)$. Again, at least one of the conditions is not satisfied.*

(c) *Contract C with terms $[A, s, \vec{P}_s]$ under which $\sum_q \pi_q V_q^s$ $(\vec{P}_s) \geq M$ and $A < \sum_q \pi_q V_q^s(\vec{P}_s)$. These are contracts similar to pooled contracts in $\Omega^C[\theta^x, M, S]$ but with lower capital. Since h's financing-NPV for each pooled contract in $\Omega^C[\theta^x, M, S]$ is less than $NPV_l^{C_h^{P_{max}}}(F)$, it follows that $NPV_h^C(F) < NPV_h^{C_h^{P_{max}}}(F)$. Thus, at least one of the conditions is not satisfied.*

(d) *Contract C with terms $[A, s, \vec{P}_s]$ under which $\sum_q \pi_q V_q^s$ $(\vec{P}_s) < M$ and $A \geq M$. These are contracts that provide $A > \sum_q \pi_q V_q^s(\vec{P}_s)$. Assume that the security s is defined by n parameters: $p_s^1 \ldots p_s^n$. Without loss of generality, $V_l^s(\vec{P}_s)$ is increasing in parameters $p_s^1 \ldots p_s^m$ and decreasing in $p_s^{m+1} \ldots p_s^n$ where $0 \leq m \leq n$. Admissible security property 4 implies that $V_h^s(\vec{P}_s)$ is also increasing in parameters $p_s^1 \ldots p_s^m$ and decreasing in $p_s^{m+1} \ldots p_s^n$.*

Increase parameters $p_s^1 \ldots p_s^m$ and/or decrease in $p_s^{m+1} \ldots p_s^n$ till a parameter $\vec{P}_s'$ is reached under which $A = \sum_q \pi_q V_q^s(\vec{P}_s')$. Label the contract with terms $[A, s, \vec{P}_s']$ as C'. This is a pooled contract and, since $A \geq M$, it is in $\Omega^C[\theta^x, M, S]$. Since l's financing-NPV is minimized under $C_h^{P_{max}}$, $NPV_l^{C'}(F) > NPV_l^{C_h^{P_{max}}}(F)$. Further since $V_q^s(\vec{P}_s)$ is increasing in $p_s^1 \ldots p_s^m$ and/or decreasing in $p_s^{m+1} \ldots p_s^n$, $V_q^s(\vec{P}_s') > V_q^s(\vec{P}_s)$ and $NPV_l^C(F) > NPV_l^{C'}(F)$. The previous two statements together yield, $NPV_l^C(F) > NPV_l^{C'}(F) > NPV_l^{C_h^{P_{max}}}(F)$. Again, at least one of the conditions is not satisfied.

Thus, no contract satisfies the two required conditions.

Part IV: No Other Contracts can be offered in equilibrium. First, consider pooled contracts other than $C_h^{P_{max}}$. Using arguments similar to those in Part III (a), it can be shown that investors can earn higher profits by offering $C_h^{P_{max}}$. Thus, no other pooled contract will be offered. Next consider no-loss contracts. Less capital is offered under a no-loss contract than under a pooled contract (see Part II). Thus, no-loss contracts are similar to those considered in Part III (c) and, using arguments similar to those in Part III (c), it can be shown that an investor will find it optimal to deviate. Thus, no-loss contracts will also not be offered.

Parts III and IV collectively demonstrate that there is a unique equilibrium in which the investors offer the $C_h^{P_{max}}$ contract.

(ii) $C_h^{\mathbf{P_{max}}}$ *is not viable for h.* This proof consists of two parts. The first part shows that only no-loss contracts *may* be offered in equilibrium and *only* firm l *may* pick an offered contract. The second part shows that no-loss contracts *will* be offered in equilibrium and the manager of firm l *will* pick any offered contract.

Part I: Only l will accept a contract and only no-loss contracts can be offered. As proven earlier, h's financing-NPV evaluated over all $\Omega^C[\theta^x, M, S]$ contracts, is maximized under the C_h^{Pmax} contract. Thus, if this contract is not viable for h, nor will any other contract in $\Omega^C[\theta^x, M, S]$. This, in turn, implies that only l will pick an offered contract.

Since only l will pick a contract, an investor offering a pooled contract will lose. This is because $NPV_l^C(F) > 0$ under all pooled contracts.

An investor will thus not offer a pooled contract. Only no-loss contracts may be offered.

Part II: No-loss Contracts will be offered and accepted. Consider the manager's choice when offered all no-loss contracts. Under these contracts, $NPV_l^C(F) = 0$. These contracts are economically viable for l and, when offered, the manager of l picks any contract randomly.

All that remains to be shown is that all no-loss contracts will be offered by the investor. To prove this, it is sufficient to show that if all no-loss contracts are offered, an investor cannot deviate and earn higher profits.

First, examine the conditions under which the investor can earn a higher profit. Suppose both investors offer the no-loss contracts. From Eq. (7d), an investor, say 1, will earn higher profits under the following possibilities: (i) he offers a $\sum_q \pi_q NPV_q^C(F) < 0$ contract and both firm-types accept the contract, (ii) he offers a $NPV_l^C(F) < 0$ contract and only l accepts the contract, and (iii) he offers a $NPV_h^C(F) < 0$ contract and only h accepts the contract,

We next show that none of these three possibilities can occur and thus no investor will deviate.

(a) *Offer C with $\sum_q \pi_q NPV_q^C(F) < 0$ and have both firm-types accept.* Since, $\sum_q \pi_q NPV_q^C(F) < 0$, the amount of capital offered under these contracts, $A < \sum_q \pi_q V_q^s(\vec{P}_s)$. These are pooled contracts in $\Omega^C[\theta^x, M, S]$ with lower A and hence lower $NPV_h^C(F)$. Since no pooled contract is viable for h, neither is C. Thus h will not accept the contract.

(b) *Offer C with $NPV_l^C(F) < 0$ and get only l to accept the contract.* Firm l will not accept this contract because it is better off accepting a no-loss contract.

(c) *Offer C with $NPV_h^C(F) < 0$ and get only h to accept the contract.* To ensure that l does not accept the contract (and accepts the no-loss contract under $NPV_l^C(F) = 0$), l must lose under contract C. Thus, for this contract $\sum_q \pi_q NPV_q^C(F) < 0$ and from (a), h will not accept this contract since it is not viable.

Since no investor can succeed in meeting these three requirements, it follows that an investor cannot deviate and earn higher profits. Thus the investor offers all no-loss contracts.

Proposition 5b. This proposition describes the equilibrium contracts set and the manager's decision when $\Omega^C[\theta^x, M, S]$ contains at least one contract with $NPV_h^C(F) = 0$ (composition 2).

It states that the equilibrium contracts set contains all pooled contracts under which $NPV_h^C(F) = NPV_l^C(F) = 0$, and all no-loss contracts. The manager of firm h chooses any pooled or no-loss contract with $NPV_h^C(F) = 0$. The manager of firm l chooses any pooled or no-loss contract with $NPV_l^C(F) = 0$.

Proof. The manager's decision under the investors' offered contracts set is straightforward and needs no explanation. What remains to be shown is that investors offer all pooled contracts under which $NPV_h^C(F) = NPV_l^C(F) = 0$ and all no-loss contracts, and that this equilibrium is unique. We do so in three parts.

The first part identifies the contracts sets (i.e., contracts/combination of contracts) in $\Omega^C[\theta^x, M, S]$ that cannot be offered. The second part shows that an investor earns zero economic profits if he offers any of the remaining contract sets. It also shows that of these, an investor *can* only offer the contracts set that contains all pooled contracts under which $NPV_h^C(F) = NPV_l^C(F) = 0$, and all no-loss contracts. The third part shows that this set *will* be offered.

Part I: Contracts sets that cannot be offered. The candidate contracts set under this composition can have five types of pooled and no-loss contracts (see proof of Proposition 4). They are a pooled $C1$ contract [under this contract $NPV_h^C(F) > 0$ and $NPV_l^C(F) < 0$], a pooled $C2$ contract [under this $NPV_h^C(F) < 0$ and $NPV_l^C(F) > 0$], a pooled $C3$ contract [under this $NPV_h^C(F) = NPV_l^C(F) = 0$], a no-loss $C4$ contract [under this $NPV_h^C(F) = 0$ and $NPV_l^C(F) < 0$] and, a no-loss $C5$ contract [under this $NPV_h^C(F) < 0$ and $NPV_l^C(F) = 0$].

The following contracts sets cannot be offered by the investor in equilibrium because either the set contains redundant contracts or the investor deviates and earns higher profits: (i) any set containing pooled $C2$ but no pooled $C1$ contracts, (ii) any set containing both pooled $C1$ and pooled $C2$ contracts, (iii) any set containing pooled $C1$ but no pooled $C2$ contracts, (iv) any set containing only no-loss $C4$ contracts, and (v) any set containing only no-loss $C5$ contracts. Consider, first, a contracts sets in category (i).

(i) *Contracts set with pooled $C2$ but no pooled $C1$ contracts.* Four possibilities arise. In each, either the contract is redundant or there is another contract that will yield higher profits for the investor.

(a) *The C2 contract is optimal for both h and l.* The firm picks the $C2$ contract from an investor at random. Firm l gains $\left[NPV_l^{C2}(F) > 0\right]$, h loses $\left[NPV_h^{C2}(F) < 0\right]$ and, each investor's expected profits $\sum_q \pi_q NPV_q^{C2}(F) = 0$. However, an investor can deviate and earn positive profits. To see this, assume that investor 1 deviates and offers a contract, C with the same terms as a pooled $C3$ contract but with ε less capital. Let $\varepsilon > NPV_h^{C2}(F)$. Under contract C, $NPV_q^{C}(F) = NPV_q^{C3}(F) - \varepsilon = -\varepsilon < 0$. That is, both firm-types lose ε. Firm l will thus still choose contract $C2$. Further, since $\varepsilon > NPV_h^{C2}(F)$, h's losses are lower under C. Thus h will choose C and the investor's expected profit, from Eq. (7c) is $\pi_h \varepsilon > 0$. This means that investor 1 will earn higher profits by deviating and offering C.

(b) *The C2 contract is optimal only for h.* A proof similar to that of Proposition 3 (case (i)(b)) shows that an investor can deviate and earn higher profits.

(c) *The C2 contract is optimal only for l.* A proof similar to that of Proposition 3 (case (i)(c)) shows that an investor can deviate and earn higher profits.

(d) *C is not optimal for h or l.* The contract is redundant.

Thus, in all four cases, an investor can either deviate and earn higher profits or the contract is redundant.

A similar analysis demonstrates the same result for contracts sets in categories (ii)–(v).

Part II: Investor profits under remaining contracts sets. The only contracts sets that remain are those with at least one pooled $C3$ contract (but no $C1$ or $C2$ contracts) or with at least one of each type of no-loss contracts, $C4$ and $C5$.

It is easily verified that an investor's expected profits are zero for each of the remaining contracts sets and that the largest set of non-redundant contracts is one with all pooled $C3$ contracts and all no-loss contracts. Thus, in equilibrium, the only contracts set that investors can offer is the set that contains all pooled $C3$ and all no-loss contracts.

Part III: Investors offer all pooled $C3$ and all no-loss contracts. If offered, investors earn zero expected profits. To prove that this set is indeed the equilibrium contracts set, it must be shown that no investor can deviate and earn higher (i.e., positive) profits. To deviate and earn positive profits, an investor must get at least one firm-type to accept a contract with a negative financing-NPV. This cannot happen because contracts with zero financing-NPV are available from the other investor. Thus, investors offer all pooled $C3$ contracts and all no-loss contracts.

Proposition 6a. This proposition considers composition 1 of the candidate contracts set under the conditions that $C_h^{P_{max}}$ is not viable for h. It states that investors offer all $NPV_l^C(F) = 0$ contracts.

Proof. When $C_h^{P_{max}}$ is not viable for h under composition 1, investors offer all no-loss contracts (see Table 1). Further, these no-loss contracts have $NPV_l^C(F) = 0$ and $NPV_h^C(F) < 0$ [Proposition 4]. To prove this proposition, it is sufficient to show that there exists no $NPV_l^C(F) = 0$ contract with $A \geq M$ and (i) $NPV_h^C(F) = 0$ or (ii) $NPV_h^C(F) > 0$.

The proof of i) is straightforward. A contract with $NPV_l^C(F) = NPV_h^C(F) = 0$ with $A \geq M$ is a pooled contract of type $C3$. However, under composition 1, such a pooled contract cannot exist (see proof of Proposition 4).

The proof of ii) is by contradiction. Suppose such a contract, C, with terms $[A, s, \vec{P_s}]$, existed. Since it is a $NPV_l^C(F) = 0$ contract with $NPV_h^C(F) > 0$ and $A \geq M$, $V_h^s(\vec{P_s}) - V_l^s(\vec{P_s}) < 0$

and $V_l^s(\vec{P}_s) = A \geq M$. Further, suppose s is defined by n parameters: $p_s^1 \dots p_s^n$. Without loss of generality, $V_l^s(\vec{P}_s)$ is increasing in parameters $p_s^1 \dots p_s^m$ and decreasing in $p_s^{m+1} \dots p_s^n$ where $0 \leq m \leq n$. Admissible security property 4 implies that $V_h^s(\vec{P}_s)$ is also increasing in parameters $p_s^1 \dots p_s^m$ and decreasing in $p_s^{m+1} \dots p_s^n$.

Using arguments similar to those in Proposition 4, Part I (iia), increasing parameters $p_s^1 \dots p_s^m$ and/or decrease in $p_s^{m+1} \dots p_s^n$ will yield a parameter $\vec{P}_s'$ under which $V_h^s(\vec{P}_s') - V_l^s(\vec{P}_s') = 0$ and $V_l^s(\vec{P}_s') > V_l^s(\vec{P}_s)$. A pooled contract under $(s, \vec{P}_s')$ will have $NPV_h^C(F) = NPV_l^C(F) = 0$. Further, the amount of capital under this pooled contract, $A' = \sum_q \pi_q V_q^s(\vec{P}_s') = V_l^s(\vec{P}_s') > V_l^s(\vec{P}_s) = A \geq M$.

Thus, if an $NPV_l^C(F) = 0$ contract exists with $NPV_h^C(F) > 0$ and $A \geq M$, there must also exist a pooled contract, $[A', s, \vec{P}_s']$, in the candidate contracts set under which $NPV_h^C(F) = NPV_l^C(F) = 0$. However, such a pooled contract does not exist under composition 1. Thus, no $NPV_l^C(F) = 0$ contract with $NPV_h^C(F) > 0$ exists.

Proposition 6b. The proposition states that irrespective of the security issued with a pooled contract, the graph of $NPV_h^C(F)$ versus A is continuous and has the same beginning and ending points.

Proof. Irrespective of the underlying security, a pooled contract satisfies three properties.

(i) ***Property 1: The maximum capital raised under pooled contracts is the pre-financing firm-value.*** With limited liability, $V_q^s(\vec{P}_s) \leq V_q^X$. Thus, from Eq. (8), it follows that the maximum capital raised under the pooled contract is $A^{Pmax} \equiv \sum_q \pi_q V_q^X$, the pre-financing firm-value.

(ii) ***Property 2: There is at least one pooled contract for each $A \in [0, A^{Pmax}]$.*** Admissible properties 2 and 4 together ensure that there is a pooled contract with some $\vec{P}_s$ that provides any amount of funds in the range $[0, A^{Pmax}]$.

To see this, assume that an admissible security, s, is defined by n parameters: $p_s^1 \ldots p_s^n$. Without loss of generality, $V_l^s(\vec{P}_s)$ is increasing in parameters $p_s^1 \ldots p_s^m$ and decreasing in $p_s^{m+1} \ldots p_s^n$ where $0 \leq m \leq n$. Admissible security property 4 implies that $V_h^s(\vec{P}_s)$ is also increasing in parameters $p_s^1 \ldots p_s^m$ and decreasing in $p_s^{m+1} \ldots p_s^n$. It follows that sufficiently reducing $p_s^1 \ldots p_s^m$ and/or increasing $p_s^{m+1} \ldots p_s^n$, will yield a $\vec{P}_s$ for which $V_q^s(\vec{P}_s) = 0 \forall q$. Under a pooled contract with terms $\vec{P}_s$, $A = 0$ [Eq. (8)]. Since $V_q^s(\vec{P}_s)$ is continuous in p_s (admissible security property 2), so is the amount of capital under a pooled contract, $A = \sum_q \pi_q V_q^s(\vec{P}_s)$. Thus, starting from $\vec{P}_s$ and increasing $p_s^1 \ldots p_s^m$ and/or decreasing $p_s^{m+1} \ldots p_s^n$ till $V_q^s(\vec{P}_s) = V_q^X \forall q$ will yield pooled contracts that provide funds in the range $(0, A^{Pmax}]$.

(iii) **Property 3: $NPV_h^C(F) = 0$ under a pooled contract that provides $A = 0$ and $NPV_h^C(F) = -\pi_l(V_h^X - V_l^X)$ when $A = A^{Pmax}$.** This proof is straightforward. As just shown, for a pooled contract with $A = 0$, $V_q^s(\vec{P}_s) = 0 \forall q$, and with $A = A^{Pmax}$, $V_q^s(\vec{P}_s) = V_q^X$. From Eq. (12a), $NPV_h^C(F) = 0$ at $A = 0$ and $NPV_h^C(F) = -\pi_l(V_h^X - V_l^X)$ at $A = A^{Pmax}$. Both are invariant to s.

These three properties together imply that, for any admissible security, a plot of $NPV_h^C(F)$ of pooled contracts against A is continuous, with the same beginning and end-points.

Proposition 8. According to this proposition, the sign of credit risk IA for $b \leq Max(X_l^\phi)$ determines whether IA is costly and costless. It states that:

(i) If credit risk IA is negative, IA is costly. For such firms, h's cost increases with increases in credit risk spread, value IA, and the firm's financing need.

(ii) If credit risk *IA* is non-negative, *IA* is costless.

(iii) If the sign of credit risk *IA* changes across b, M determines whether *IA* is costless or costly. For such firms

- *IA* is costless (costly) when M is small (large) and
- The likelihood that *IA* is costless (costly) is non-decreasing (non-increasing) in credit risk *IA* and non-increasing (non-decreasing) in value *IA*.

Proof. Consider each of the three cases separately.

(i) **Negative credit risk IA for $b \leq Max(X_l^\phi)$.** This proof consists of two parts. The first part shows that *IA* is costly for these firms and the second part shows that the magnitude of this cost is large when credit risk spread, value *IA*, and the firm's financing needs are large.

Part I: IA is costly. To prove this part, it is sufficient to show that $\Omega^C[\theta^x, M, S]$ only contains $NPV_h^C(F) < 0$ contracts (Table 1). When credit risk *IA* is negative, $NPV_h^C(F) < 0$ for debt and debt–equity contracts [see discussion following Eqs. (14) and (16b)]. Also, $NPV_h^C(F) < 0$ for equity contracts [see discussion following Eq. (15)]. Thus, $NPV_h^C(F) < 0$ for all contracts in $\Omega^C[\theta^x, M, S]$.

Part II: Magnitude of h's cost. To prove this part it is necessary to examine $NPV_h^C(F)$ under the C_h^{Pmax} contract (the contract chosen by the firm); the more negative the $NPV_h^C(F)$, the larger is h's cost of raising capital.

When M is large, there are fewer pooled contracts in the candidate contracts set. This implies that $NPV_h^C(F)$ under the C_h^{Pmax} contract is more negative and hence, h's cost is larger.

The greater the magnitude of credit risk *IA* (credit risk spread) and value *IA*, the more negative is $NPV_h^C(F)$ of all pooled contracts [see discussion following Eqs. (14), (15), and (16b)]. Thus, $NPV_h^C(F)$ under the $C_h^{P_{max}}$ contract is also more negative.

(ii) **Non-negative credit risk IA for $b \leq Max(X_l^\phi)$.** The proof again consists of two parts. The first part shows that *IA* is costless when credit risk *IA* is zero and the second part shows *IA* is costless when credit risk *IA* is positive.

Part I: Credit risk IA is zero. To prove *IA* is costless, it is sufficient to show that $\Omega^C[\theta^x, M, S]$ also contains a $NPV_h^C(F) = 0$ contract (Table 1). That is, there is at least one pooled or no-loss contract with $NPV_h^C(F) = 0$ and $A \geq M$.

Consider the debt pooled contract at $b = Max(X_l^\phi)$. Since credit risk *IA* is zero, $NPV_h^C(F) = 0$ under the contract.

Further, at this b, $X_l^\phi(s, \vec{P}_s) = X_l^\phi \forall \phi$ and thus, $V_l^s(\vec{P}_s) = V_l^X$. Since credit risk *IA* is zero, $V_h^s(\vec{P}_s) = V_l^X$. The pooled contract therefore provides $A = \sum_q \pi_q V_q^s(\vec{P}_s) = V_l^X$. Since $V_l^X \geq M$, it follows $A \geq M$.

Thus, the debt pooled contract at $b = Max(X_l^\phi)$ has $NPV_h^C(F) = 0$ and $A \geq M$.

Part II: Credit risk IA is Positive. Again, consider the debt pooled contract at $b = Max(X_l^\phi)$. At this b, again, $V_l^s(\vec{P}_s) = V_l^X$. Since credit risk *IA* is positive, $V_h^s(\vec{P}_s) < V_l^s(\vec{P}_s) = V_l^X$. As b increases, $V_l^s(\vec{P}_s)$ remains constant (limited liability) but $V_h^s(\vec{P}_s)$ increases. At some $b = b'$, $V_h^s(\vec{P}_s) = V_l^X$. Now both $V_l^s(\vec{P}_s)$ and $V_h^s(\vec{P}_s)$ are equal to V_l^X at $b = b'$. Thus, under this pooled contract, $NPV_h^C(F) = 0$ [Eq. (12a)] and $A = \sum_q \pi_q V_q^s(\vec{P}_s) = V_l^X \geq M$.

(iii) **Sign of credit risk IA changes.** The arguments in this proof thus far also show that when the sign of credit risk *IA* changes, M determines whether there is a $NPV_h^C(F) = 0$

contract in $\Omega^C[\theta^x, M, S]$ or not. If M is sufficiently small, there are many contracts in the candidate contracts set and there will be at least one debt or debt–equity contract under which $NPV_h^C(F) = 0$. Thus, IA is costless when M is small.

Further, higher credit risk IA and lower value IA increase the probability that $\Omega^C[\theta^x, M, S]$ contains a debt contract with non-negative credit risk IA or a debt–equity contract with $R^{DE}(\theta^x, b, f) = 0$ [see discussion following Eqs. (14) and (16b)]. This, in turn, increases the possibility that there is at least one $NPV_h^C(F) = 0$ contract in $\Omega^C[\theta^x, M, S]$ and hence the likelihood that IA is costless.

Proposition 10a. According to this proposition, the impact of M on the security associated with the $C_h^{P_{max}}$ contract (the contract chosen by the firm) depends on θ^x. It states that:

(i) If $R^\varphi(\theta^x, b) > 0$ at low b and $R^\varphi(\theta^x, b) < 0$ at high b, the security associated with the $C_h^{P_{max}}$ contract is debt (equity) if M is high (low).

(ii) If $R^\varphi(\theta^x, b) < 0$ at low b and $R^\varphi(\theta^x, b) > 0$ at high b, the security associated with the $C_h^{P_{max}}$ contract is debt–equity (debt) if M is high (low).

Proof. Consider (i) and (ii) separately.

(i) $R^\varphi(\theta^x, b) > 0$ *at low b and* $R^\varphi(\theta^x, b) < 0$ *at high* b. To identify the security associated with the $C_h^{P_{max}}$ contract, it is necessary to examine the graph of financing-NPV of pooled contracts with $NPV_h^C(F)$ on the y-axis and the amount of capital on the x-axis. Note the following:

- Since the sign of $R^\varphi(\theta^x, b) \equiv \varphi_h(\tilde{X}_h, b) - \varphi_l(\tilde{X}_l, b)$ is first positive and then negative, the graph is convexo-concave in A for debt pooled contracts [Eq. (17b)]. The beginning point of this graph is the origin and the end point is $A = A^{Pmax}$ and $NPV_h^C(F) = -\pi_l(V_h^X - V_l^X)$ [Proposition 6b].

- The graph is linear and decreasing in A for equity pooled contracts [Eq. (18)]. The beginning point of this graph is also the origin and the end point is $A = A^{Pmax}$ and $NPV_h^C(F) = -\pi_l(V_h^X - V_l^X)$ [Proposition 6b].
- As discussed prior to Proposition 9, for all debt–equity contracts with the same face value, say b_1

  o The graph is linear.
  o The beginning point of the graph is for the debt–equity contract with $f = 0$. It is the point on the curve of the debt pooled contracts with face value b_1.
  o The ending point of the graph is again $A = A^{Pmax}$ and $NPV_h^C(F) = -\pi_l(V_h^X - V_l^X)$. Note that the endpoint is independent of b_1.

Collectively, the preceding discussion implies that debt (equity) maximizes h's financing-NPV if M is high (low).

(ii) $R^\varphi(\theta^x, b) < 0$ at low b and $R^\varphi(\theta^x, b) > 0$ at high b.
The discussion regarding the graph is the same as in (i) except that the graph for $NPV_h^C(F)$ is concavo-convex in A for debt pooled contracts. As a result, now, debt–equity (debt) maximizes h's financing-NPV if M is high (low).

Proposition 10c. This proposition states that firms with high risk and those for which a greater proportion of value IA comes from downside IA are more likely to choose a contract that contains equity (either with or without debt).

Proof. The firm is more likely to choose a contract that contains equity (either with or without debt) if credit risk spread is large (Proposition 10b). This means that to prove this proposition it is sufficient to show that firms with high risk and large downside IA have greater credit risk spread.

We prove this in a binomial world in order to obtain closed-form solutions. Since h is the higher-valued firm with lower credit risk and we are examining the case where the sign of hazard rate changes, it follows that θ^x must satisfy the following condition: $X_l^d < X_h^d < X_l^u < X_h^u$. The proof has three parts.

Part I: The only relevant credit risk spreads are for $b \leq X_l^u$. To show this result it is sufficient to show that the firm never chooses a debt contract with $b > X_l^u$. Consider the debt pooled contract at $b = X_l^u$. Under this contract, $A = \sum_q \pi_q V_q^D(b) > V_l^X > M$. This pooled contract is thus in the candidate contracts set. Further, h's financing-NPV under debt pooled contracts decrease as b increases beyond X_l^u. The previous two statements, in conjunction with the fact that the firm chooses the $C_h^{P_{max}}$ contract, imply that it will never choose a debt contract with $b > X_l^u$.

Part II: Firms with larger risk have larger credit risk spread for $b \leq X_l^u$. To show this result, it is sufficient to show that either h's credit risk decreases or l's increases when risk of the firm's cash flows increases. An increase in the risk of the firm's cash flows decreases X_l^d and X_h^d while increasing X_l^u and X_h^u. Hence, for all $b \leq X_l^d$, h's and l's credit risk remain the same and credit risk spread remains unaffected. For all $X_l^d < b \leq X_h^d$, h's credit risk remains the same but l's credit risk increases because l makes lower payments to the investor in default (and thus the investor loses more). Thus, credit risk spread increases. For all $X_h^d < b \leq X_l^u$, h's and l's credit risk increases by the same amount since an increase in risk has the same effect on the cash flows of both types and thus the payments made by both in default decrease by the same amount. Thus, credit risk spread remains unaffected. Summarizing, an increase in risk increases credit risk spread for $X_l^d < b \leq X_h^d$ (while leaving it unchanged for the remaining face values of debt).

Part III: *Firms for which a greater proportion of value IA comes from the downside IA have higher credit spreads for $b \leq X_i^u$.* Downside *IA* is measured by $X_h^d - X_l^d$. A larger downside *IA* implies that either X_l^d is lower and/or X_h^d is higher. The proof of Part II implies that the credit risk spread will be larger for $X_l^d < b \leq X_h^d$ (while leaving it unchanged for the remaining face values of debt).

The three parts collectively imply that credit risk spread is higher for firms with high risk and those for which a larger proportion of value *IA* comes from the downside *IA*.

Proposition 11a. This proposition identifies the range of financing choices for h and l when *IA* is costless. Firm h issues: (i) debt contracts with $R^D(\theta^x, b) = 0$ or $R^D(\theta^x, b) < 0$ or (ii) debt–equity contracts with $f \leq \bar{f} = R^D(\theta^x, b)/[R^D(\theta^x, b) - (V_h^X - V_l^X)]$. Firm l issues: (i) debt contracts with $R^D(\theta^x, b) = 0$, (ii) equity contracts, or (iii) debt–equity contracts with $f \geq \bar{f} = R^D(\theta^x, b)/[R^D(\theta^x, b) - (V_h^X - V_l^X)]$.

Proof. The range of financing choices for h is determined by the $(s, \vec{P_s})$ of the pooled and no-loss contract with $NPV_h^C(F) = 0$ and $NPV_l^C(F) \leq 0$ (see Table 1). The only pooled contracts that satisfy this condition are those with $NPV_h^C(F) = NPV_l^C(F) = 0$. As in the proof of Proposition 4, denote such pooled contracts as pooled $C3$ contracts. The only no-loss contracts that satisfy this condition are ones with $NPV_h^C(F) = 0$ and $NPV_l^C(F) < 0$ (denoted as no-loss $C4$ contracts).

Similarly, the range of financing choices for l is determined by the $(s, \vec{P_s})$ of the pooled and no-loss contract with $NPV_l^C(F) = 0$ and $NPV_h^C(F) \leq 0$ (see Table 1). The only pooled contracts that satisfy this condition are pooled $C3$ contracts. Similarly, the only no-loss contracts that satisfy this condition are ones with $NPV_l^C(F) = 0$ and $NPV_h^C(F) < 0$ (denoted as no-loss $C5$ contracts).

Thus, to prove this proposition, it is sufficient to identify the $(s, \vec{P}_s)$ of all pooled $C3$ contracts and all no-loss $C4$ and $C5$ contracts. We begin with pooled $C3$ contracts. Consider each of the three securities separately.

(i) *Equity*: $NPV_h^C(F) < 0$ for all equity contracts [see discussion following Eq. (15)]. Thus, there are no equity pooled $C3$ contracts.

(ii) *Debt*: The debt pooled $C3$ contract are ones with $R^D(\theta^x, b) = 0$ [see discussion following Eq. (14)].

(iii) *Debt–Equity*. The debt–equity pooled $C3$ contracts are those with $R^{DE}(\theta^x, b, f) = 0$ [see discussion following Eq. (16b)]. Substituting $R^E(\theta^x, f)$ from Eq. (15) into (16b) and re-arranging yields that $R^{DE}(\theta^x, b, f) = 0$ if the fraction of equity, $f = \bar{f} \equiv R^D(\theta^x, b)/[R^D(\theta^x, b) - (V_h^X - V_l^X)]$. Thus, the only debt–equity pooled $C3$ contracts are those with $f = \bar{f}$.

Repeating a similar process determines the $(s, \vec{P}_s)$ of the no-loss $C4$ and $C5$ contracts. Collectively, these results show that h chooses debt contracts or debt–equity contracts with $f \leq \bar{f}$ and l chooses debt contracts with $R^D(\theta^x, b) = 0$, equity contracts, or debt–equity with $f \geq \bar{f}$.

Proposition 11b. This proposition states that the greater the credit risk spread and/or the lower the value IA due to lower (higher) cash flow for $h(l)$, the greater is the amount of equity contained in the firm's chosen debt–equity contract.

Proof. The amount of equity in the chosen debt–equity contract is an increasing function of $\bar{f}$ (see discussion prior to Proposition 11b). To prove this proposition, it is thus sufficient to show that $\bar{f}$ increases when: (i) credit risk spread increases and (ii) value *IA* decreases. Consider each of the two parts separately.

(i) *Credit Risk Spread*: Note that credit risk spread determines $|R^D(\theta^x, b)|$; the larger the credit risk spread, the greater is $|R^D(\theta^x, b)|$. To determine the impact that credit risk spread has on $\bar{f}$, it is sufficient to determine the impact of $|R^D(\theta^x, b)|$. With $V_h^X - V_l^X > 0$ and $\frac{\partial R^D(\theta^x, b)}{\partial |R^D(\theta^x, b)|} = -1$ [since we are considering firms with $R^D(\theta^x, b) < 0$], it follows that

$$\frac{\partial \bar{f}}{\partial |R^D(\theta^x, b)|} = \frac{\partial \bar{f}}{\partial R^D(\theta^x, b)} * \frac{\partial R^D(\theta^x, b)}{\partial |R^D(\theta^x, b)|}$$

$$= \frac{-(V_h^X - V_l^X)}{[R^D(\theta^x, b) - (V_h^X - V_l^X)]^2}(-1) > 0.$$

Therefore, as $|R^D(\theta^x, b)|$ increases, $\bar{f}$ increases.

(ii) *Value IA*. Note that

$$\frac{\partial \bar{f}}{\partial (V_h^X - V_l^X)}$$

$$= \frac{R^D(\theta^x, b) - (V_h^X - V_l^X) * \partial R^D(\theta^x, b)/\partial(V_h^X - V_l^X)}{[R^D(\theta^x, b) - (V_h^X - V_l^X)]^2}.$$

If value *IA* increases because of an increase (decrease) in $h's$ ($l's$) cash flows in one, some, or all states of the economy, $R^D(\theta^x, b)$ also increases. That is, $\partial R(D)/\partial(V_h^X - V_l^X) > 0$. Also, since we are considering firms for which credit risk *IA* is positive, $R^D(\theta^x, b) < 0$. The previous statements yield that $\frac{\partial \bar{f}}{\partial(V_h^X - V_l^X)} < 0$. Thus, as value *IA* decreases, $\bar{f}$ increases.

Proposition 11c. This proposition states that firms with high risk and a large magnitude of downside *IA* choose debt–equity contracts with a larger amounts of equity.

Proof. If credit risk spread is large or value *IA* is small, firms choose debt–equity contracts with a larger amount of equity

(Proposition 11b). To prove this proposition it is sufficient to show that firms with high risk and large magnitude downside *IA* have greater credit risk spread or lower value *IA*.

To obtain closed form solutions, we again prove the result in a binomial world. Since h is the higher-valued firm and we are examining the case where h has the same or higher credit risk than l, it follows that θ^x satisfies the following condition: $X_h^d < X_l^d < X_l^u < X_h^u$. The proof has two parts.

Part I: Firms with larger risk have larger credit risk spread. To show this result, it is sufficient to show that either h's credit risk increases or l's decreases when risk of the firm's cash flows increases. An increase in the risk of the firm's cash flows decreases X_l^d and X_h^d while increasing X_l^u and X_h^u. Hence, for all $b \le X_h^d$, h's and l's credit risk remains the same and credit risk spread remains unaffected. For all $X_h^d < b \le X_l^d$, l's credit risk remains the same but h's increases because h makes lower payments to the investor in default (and thus the investor loses more). Thus, credit risk spread increases. For all $X_l^d < b \le X_l^u$, h's and l's credit risk increases by the same amount since an increase in risk has the same effect on the cash flows of both types and thus the payments made by both in default decrease by the same amount. Thus, credit risk spread remains unaffected. For all $X_l^u < b \le X_h^u$, h defaults only in the downside while l defaults in the upside and the downside. Here h's credit risk increases because it makes lower payments in the downside. However, l's credit risk is unaffected since the decrease in its payments in the downside is exactly offset by the increase in payments on the upside (l's expected cash flows are unaffected; only the risk changes). Thus, credit risk spread increases. Clearly, an increase in risk increases credit risk spread for $X_h^d < b \le X_l^d$ and for $X_l^u < b \le X_h^u$ (while leaving it unchanged for the remaining face values of debt).

**Part II: Firms with larger magnitude of downside IA
(i.e., magnitude of $X_l^d - X_h^d$) have higher credit spreads
and lower value IA.** A larger magnitude of downside IA
implies that either X_l^d is higher and/or X_h^d is lower. This means
that either the value of l is higher or the value of h is lower,
i.e., IA about value is lower. Further, the analysis in the proof
of Part I implies that the credit risk spread will be larger for
$X_h^d < b \le X_l^d$ (while leaving it unchanged for the remaining face
values of debt).

The two parts collectively imply that firms with high risk
and larger downside IA have a higher credit risk spread and/or
lower value IA.

Proposition 12. This proposition states that when S is
expanded to include admissible securities that complete the markets, IA becomes costless for all firms.

Proof. IA is costless when $\Omega^C[\theta^x, M, S]$ contains a $NPV_h^C(F) =
0$ contract (see Table 1). Thus, to prove this proposition, it is
sufficient to demonstrate that when markets are complete, there
exists a $NPV_h^C(F) = 0$ contract with $A \ge M$ for all firms.
Consider the following two mutually exclusive but exhaustive
cases.

(i) **Firms for which the cash flows of h exceed and/or
equal those of l in each state of the world.** Assume
there are Φ states of the world. Define a "complete market security" (i.e., $s = AD$) as a combination of all Φ per-
fectly divisible Arrow–Debreu securities. A complete market
security is described by Φ parameters, i.e., $\vec{P}_s = [p_1 p_2, \dots,
p_\phi, \dots, p_\Phi]$ where p_ϕ takes a non-negative value and denotes
the payoff of the complete market security in state ϕ.[2] With

---

[2]Thus, if there are three states of the world and $\vec{P}_s = [2, 0, 3]$, the security
promises to pay \$2 in the first state, zero dollars in the second state and
\$3 in the third state.

complete markets, a complete markets security will exist. Since the payoffs of firm h exceed (or are equal to) those of l in each state, it follows that there will be a $\vec{P}_s$ under which: $X_h^\phi(AD, \vec{P}_s) = X_l^\phi(AD, \vec{P}_s) = X_l^\phi$ in each state. Thus, a pooled contract under $s = AD$ will:

- Provide $A = \sum_q \pi_q V_q^{AD}(\vec{P}_s) = V_l^X \geq M$ in capital, and
- have $V_h^{AD}(\vec{P}_s) = V_l^{AD}(\vec{P}_s) = V_l^X$ and hence $NPV_h^C(F) = 0$ [Eq. (12a)].

(ii) **Firms for which the cash flows of h are less than those of l in some states of the world.** Consider a pooled contract with $s = ADE$, i.e., the aforementioned complete market security (i.e., $s = AD$) as the senior security and equity with $f = \frac{V_l^X - V_h^{AD}(\vec{P}_s)}{V_h^X - V_h^{AD}(\vec{P}_s)}$ as the junior security (The complete market security has a $\vec{P}_s$ under which $X_l^\phi(AD, \vec{P}_s) = X_l^\phi$. Further, if actual equity does not trade, synthetic equity can be designed and issued in complete markets). For the senior Arrow–Debreu securities, $V_l^{AD}(\vec{P}_s) = V_l^X$ but $V_h^{AD}(\vec{P}_s) < V_l^X$, (since cash flows of h are less than those of l in some states of the world). Under $s = ADE$, it can easily be verified that $V_h^{ADE}(\vec{P}_s) = V_l^{ADE}(\vec{P}_s) = V_l^X$. Thus, the pooled contract with $s = ADE$ has $A \geq M$ and $NPV_h^C(F) = 0$

Hence, in both cases, $\Omega^C[\theta^x, M, S]$ contains a $NPV_h^C(F) = 0$ contract.

References

Akbulut, M.E. and J.G. Matsusaka, 2010, "50 + Years of Diversification Announcements," *The Financial Review* 45, 231–262.

Akerlof, G.A., 1970, "The Market for 'Lemons': Quality Uncertainty and the Market Mechanism," *Quarterly Journal of Economics* 488–500.

Axelson, U., 2007, "Security Design with Investor Private Information," *Journal of Finance* 62, 2587–2631.

Baker, M. and J. Wurgler, 2002, "Market Timing and Capital Structure," *Journal of Finance* 57, 1–32.

Breeden, D. and S. Viswanathan, 1998, "Why Do Firms Hedge? An Asymmetric Information Model," Working Paper, Fuqua School of Business, Duke University.

Brennan, M., 1995, "Corporate Finance Over the Past 25 Years," *Financial Management* 24, 9–22.

Brennan, M. and A. Kraus, 1987, "Efficient Financing under Asymmetric Information," *Journal of Finance* 42, 225–243.

Chakraborty, A., S. Gervais and B. Yilmaz, 2011, "Security Design in Initial Public Offerings," *Review of Finance* 15, 327–357.

Comment, R. and G.A. Jarrell, 1995, "Corporate Focus and Stock Returns," *Journal of Financial Economics* 37, 67–87.

Constantinides, G.M. and B.D. Grundy, 1989, "Optimal Investment with Stock Repurchase and Financing as Signals," *Review of Financial Studies* 2, 445–465.

DeMarzo, P.M. and D. Duffie, 1991, "Corporate Financial Hedging with Proprietary Information," *Journal of Economic Theory* 53, 261–286.

Dybvig, P.H. and J.F. Zender, 1991, "Capital Structure and Dividend Irrelevance with Asymmetric Information," *Review of Financial Studies* 4, 201–219.

Fama, E. and K. French, 1992, "The Cross-section of Expected Stock Returns," *Journal of Finance* 47, 427–465.

Fama, E. and K.R. French, 2002, "Testing Trade-Off and Pecking Order Predictions about Dividends and Debt," *Review of Financial Studies* 15, 35–64.

Fama, E. and K.R. French, 2005, "Financing Decisions: Who Issues Stock?," *Journal of Financial Economics* 76, 549–582.

Frank, M. and V.K. Goyal, 2003, "Testing the Pecking Order Theory of Capital Structure," *Journal of Financial Economics* 67, 217–248.

Frank, M. and V.K. Goyal, 2005, "Trade-off and Pecking Order Theories of Debt," in B. Espen Eckbo, ed.: *Handbook of Corporate Finance: Empirical Corporate Finance.* Elsevier: North-Holland.

Froot, K., D. Scharfstein and J. Stein, 1993, "Risk Management: Coordinating Corporate Investment and Financing Policies," *Journal of Finance* 48, 1629–1658.

Fulghieri, P. and D. Lukin, 2001, "Information Production, Dilution Costs, and Optimal Security Design," *Journal of Financial Economics* 61, 3–42.

Gale, D., 1992, "Standard Securities," *The Review of Economic Studies* 59, 731–755.

Garcia, D., P. Fulghieri and D. Hackbarth, 2013, "Asymmetric Information and the Pecking (Dis)Order," Working Paper.

Giammarino, R.M. and E.F. Neave, 1982, "The Failure of Financial Contracts and the Relevance of Financial Policy," Working Paper, Queen's University.

Graham, J.R. and C.R. Harvey, 2001, "The Theory and Practice of Corporate Finance: Evidence from the Field," *Journal of Financial Economics* 60, 187–243.

Graham, J.R. and D.A. Rogers, 2002, "Do Firms Hedge in Response to Tax Incentives?," *Journal of Finance* 57, 815–839.

Harris, M. and A. Raviv, 1989, "The Design of Securities," *Journal of Financial Economics* 24, 255–287.

Harris, M. and A. Raviv, 1991, "The Theory of Capital Structure," *Journal of Finance* 46, 297–355.

Heinkel, R., 1982, "A Theory of Capital Structure Relevance under Imperfect Information," *Journal of Finance* 37, 1141–1150.

Hennessy, C.A., D. Livdan and B. Miranda, 2010, "Repeated Signaling and Firm Dynamics," *Review of Financial Studies* 23, 1981–2023.

Hovakimian, A., G. Hovakimian and H. Tehranian, 2004, "Determinants of Target Capital Structure: The Case of Dual Debt and Equity Issues," *Journal of Financial Economics* 71, 517–540.

Innes, R.D., 1993, "Financial Contracting under Risk Neutrality, Limited Liability and *Ex ante* Asymmetric Information," *Economica* 60, 27–40.

Jung, K., Y. Kim and R.M. Stulz, 1996, "Timing, Investment Opportunities, Managerial Discretion, and the Security Issue Decision," *Journal of Financial Economics* 42, 159–185.

Kayhan, A. and S. Titman, 2007, "Firms' Histories and their Capital Structures," *Journal of Financial Economics* 83, 1–32.

Leary, T. and M.R. Roberts, 2006, "The Pecking Order, Debt Capacity, and Information Asymmetry," Working Paper, Duke University and Wharton Business School.

Lemmon, M. and J. Zender, 2010, "Debt Capacity and Tests of Capital Structure Theories," *Journal of Financial and Quantitative Analysis* 45, 1161–1187.

Milgrom, P.R., 1981, "Good News and Bad News: Representation Theorems and Applications," *Bell Journal of Economics* 12, 380–391.

Morellec, E. and N. Schürhoff, 2011, "Corporate Investment and Financing Under Asymmetric Information," *Journal of Financial Economics* 2, 262–288.

Modigliani, F. and M.H. Miller, 1958, "The Cost of Capital, Corporation Finance and the Theory of Investment," *American Economic Review* 48, 261–297.

Myers, S.C., 1984, "The Capital Structure Puzzle," *Journal of Finance* 39, 575–592.

Myers, S.C., 2001, "Capital Structure," *The Journal of Economic Perspectives* 15, 81–102.

Myers, S.C. and N.S. Majluf, 1984, "Corporate Financing and Investment Decisions when Firms have Information that Investors do not have," *Journal of Financial Economics* 13, 187–221.

Nachman, D. and T. Noe, 1994, "Optimal Design of Securities under Asymmetric Information," *Review of Financial Studies* 7, 1–44.

Noe, T.H., 1988, "Capital Structure and Signaling Game Equilibria," *Review of Financial Studies* 1, 331–355.

Opler, T., L. Pinkowitz, R. Stulz and R. Williamson, 1999, "The Determinants and Implications of Corporate Cash Holdings," *Journal of Financial Economics* 52, 3–46.

Rothschild, M. and J. Stiglitz, 1976, "Equilibrium in Competitive Insurance Markets: An Essay on the Economics of Imperfect Information," *Quarterly Journal of Economics* 629–650.

Shyam-Sunder, L. and S.C. Myers, 1999, "Testing Static Tradeoff Against Pecking Order Models of Capital Structure," *Journal of Financial Economics* 51, 219–244.

Tang, T.T., 2009, "Information Asymmetry and Firms' Credit Market Access: Evidence from Moody's Credit Rating Format Refinement," *Journal of Financial Economics* 93, 325–351.

Titman, S., and R. Wessels, 1988, "The Determinants of Capital Structure Choice," *Journal of Finance* 43, 1–19.

Tirole, J., 2006, *The Theory of Corporate Finance*, Princeton University Press: New Jersey.

Tufano, P., 2003, "Financial Innovation" in G. Constantinides, M. Harris and R.M. Stulz (eds.): *Handbook of the Economics of Finance*, Vol. 1A. Elsevier.

Index